Puzzle Pieces

Books by Vikki Carrel
Chloe's Closet
Switching Lanes
Puzzle Pieces

Puzzle Pieces

A practical approach to successful living:
Strategies to move from ordinary to extraordinary

VIKKI CARREL

Puzzle Pieces

Editing: Jodi Goodman
Final editing: Connie Weissinger Tucker, Eschler Editing
Cover design: Rochelle Tolman
Book design: The Printed Page

ISBN: 978-0-9761861-2-0

Published by Beaman Company, LLC

Dedication

A friend is one that knows you, understands where you have been, accepts what you have become, and still encourages you to grow.

This book is dedicated to my friends—the individuals in my life who have loved the best in me and chosen to overlook my weaknesses, accepting me for who I am and encouraging me to be better, stronger, and happier.

Over the years I have met many people, lived in several places, and done a fair amount of traveling. These opportunities have prompted me to make friends with individuals who have different perspectives than my own, teaching me life-changing lessons. Belonging to a group of good friends as a teenager and throughout adulthood has made all the difference for me. I am blessed to have friends that encourage me to understand myself, accept what I have become, and strive for continued personal and professional growth.

Fortunately, I remain connected to many of my childhood friends. One of them is Lisa. She rescued me from a group of girls in the seventh grade who found it entertaining and empowering to bully me. Lisa saw beyond my awkwardness and insecurities. We were in several classes together that year and quickly became best friends. Lisa has taught me many life lessons. The insight I value most, is to be still, listen, and in a world full of commotion, to follow my instincts.

My adulthood friends live across the United States. Our paths crossed for a time and then we moved on to new places and opportunities. Over the years these friends helped me navigate new cities, find the perfect home in a friendly neighborhood, embrace motherhood, thrive in various community organizations, raise our two boys, and succeed professionally.

Shortly after marrying my husband, Jeff, we moved to Sacramento, California where he trained to be a navigator for the United States Air Force. Following eighteen months of training in California, Jeff was stationed at Ellsworth Air Force Base in Rapid City, South Dakota. What an adventure this was for Jeff and me, both personally and professionally. It was during this time that I met Vicki, a bright, talented, enthusiastic woman. Together we opened a dance studio and modeling agency. Vicki was an accomplished ballerina, and I had experience in fashion show production as a runway show choreographer. The success of our business was largely due to Vicki's business experience and insights. She taught me the importance of focus and clarity—to have a vision, execute a plan, and believe!

Following Jeff's commitment to the Air Force, he was hired by McNeil Consumer Products, a subsidiary of Johnson and Johnson. Debbi is one of the first women I connected with after my husband and I moved to Austin, Texas. We became close friends and business partners. Debbi helped me learn to appreciate my talents and abilities as an entrepreneur and to thrive as a working mom. She supported me as I navigated my way through the stresses of motherhood. Debbi rescued me on numerous occasions when I was overwhelmed by the day-to-day tasks of mothering and the demands of our growing business. Debbi encouraged me to see the best in myself by recognizing the essentials in life and learning to "let go" of the nonessentials.

After living over a decade in Texas and learning to love the area and lifestyle, my husband got a promotion, and we moved to a suburb of Philadelphia. I felt extremely overwhelmed by this move, the sale of my Texas-based fashion production company, and the lack of friends. I felt paralyzed personally and professionally. Shortly after moving to the East, I became pregnant and had some health issues due to the pregnancy. Living in a new state, a new neighborhood and spending most of my days in bed while trying to care for our busy three-year-old son were daunting and extremely difficult.

Through my church group, I met Lynn, an amazing woman, willing to serve others at a moment's notice. She instantly recognized my need for help, support, and friendship. Again, another friend rescued me. Lynn brought in meals, took my son on outings and drove me to the doctor when I was too sick to drive myself. She saw an opportunity to serve and love, and through it all we became close friends. We have raised children together, buried parents, cried over life's tragedies, and celebrated life's successes. Lynn taught me unconditional love and that service is a strong predictor of happiness.

Joe is a friend from college and was in the Air Force ROTC program with my husband at The University of Utah. Our paths crossed years ago, and they continue to cross today. Joe is a brilliant man with a huge heart. He has cheered me on from the sidelines for years. Joe rescued me on a cold November day when I was attempting to prepare my first Thanksgiving dinner away from home. He encouraged me and applauded me as I struggled to balance it all—from preparing the turkey to cooking the yams and making the gravy. We laughed a lot that day. With Joe's help, support, and sense of humor my first Thanksgiving meal was a success. He taught me the importance of optimism—to look at the glass half-full and not half-empty.

I love the quote by Albert Camus, "Don't walk behind me; I may not lead. Don't walk in front of me; I may not follow. Just walk beside me and be my friend."

Thank you to all my friends who have walked beside me, shared their time and insights, rescued me when I needed rescuing and provided me with endless hours of sheer joy.

This book is filled with lessons I have learned from all my friends who have crossed my path over the many years. To each of them let me say *thank you* for taking the time to teach me how to build confidence, feel capable and live a successful life.

Contents

PUZZLE PIECES

Author's Note

The entries of this book are a collection of my blog posts, articles, interviews, and presentations from past years. Contained in each entry are lessons learned over a lifetime.

Insights from hundreds of conversations with family, friends, and colleagues have contributed to the content of this book. Puzzle Pieces is a collection of information shared by personal and professional friends, researchers, and scholars who have taken the time to teach and inspire me. Their contributions have made this project possible, and I offer sincere thanks for their support.

What started as a single blog post or interview has resulted in my attempt to share strategies and tools necessary to complete one's "life puzzle" and live a successful life.

It is impossible to name all those individuals who have contributed to the content of these pages. I would like to have credited all for their contributions, but for the sake of readability I will list only those individuals who reviewed my manuscript.

Debbie Carrel   Diana Sackett
Kabi Catalano   Lynn Schoendorfer
Vicki Draxton   Bette Taylor
Julie Kane   Jane Thomas
Joseph B. Michels, PhD.   Rebecca Warren

Introduction

Putting together a jigsaw puzzle is a process. While visiting my eighty-four-year-old mother at the retirement community where she lives, I often observe elderly men and women enjoying puzzles. I am amazed by their ability to concentrate and intently work for hours building a 1,000-piece puzzle. My mom explains to me, "Puzzles sharpen thinking skills and keep our brains working." I chuckle to myself as she states the reasoning behind the puzzle building process. For me, getting started is overwhelming due to the numerous small pieces. I ask myself, will the puzzle really come together and look like the picture on the front of the box?

The key to putting together a puzzle is to get started. It begins with one piece. First, I find the corners of the puzzle because they are easy to identify. Mom begins by organizing all the puzzle pieces by color, and my niece, Mattison, starts by putting together the outer perimeter of the puzzle and then works toward the center. I have seen Mattison spend several weeks completing a 5,000-piece puzzle. Puzzle building is a process, it's different for each of us, and yet it's about finding and placing one puzzle piece at a time.

Have you ever been disappointed at the end of the process when you discover that two or three pieces of the puzzle are missing? Discouragement sets in because the puzzle picture is incomplete.

All that work placing each piece only to feel a lack of accomplishment in the end.

Daily living is similar to putting together a puzzle; it is also a process. You strive to accomplish tasks, meet deadlines, and feel happy. You work on completing your "personal puzzle" by building it one piece at a time. In the end, you hope that the picture will be beautiful, leaving you with feelings of accomplishment and joy.

Each day is different with various challenges and rewards. At the end of some days you feel that life has fallen short of your expectations leaving you with feelings of frustration, exhaustion, and limited joy. Other days run smoothly and, as you climb into bed at night, you feel a sense of accomplishment and happiness. When you step back, observe your life and the way you choose to live each day, do you see pieces missing from your "personal puzzle" that leave holes in your picture of life?

What pieces are missing from your "personal puzzle" that are causing you to feel discouraged, overwhelmed, lacking clarity, and unable to focus? As you read this book, you will *build confidence* in yourself, *feel capable* about your talents and abilities, and increase optimism in order to *achieve success*.

As you identify the missing puzzle pieces in your life, recognize this process as an opportunity to improve yourself and boost your self-esteem. Missing pieces should not create negative feelings or remind you of past failures. We all have missing puzzle pieces. It's what we choose to do about it that allows us to grow. Stay positive, allowing this process to empower you and to identify what's missing in your life. May the insights, tools and strategies contained on the pages of this book help you complete your "personal puzzle," live a fulfilled life, and to feel joy.

Build Confidence

I think that the power is the principle. The principle of moving forward, as though you have the confidence to move forward, eventually gives you confidence when you look back and see what you've done.

-Robert Downey, Jr.

PUZZLE PIECES IN THIS SECTION:

Build Confidence One Puzzle Piece at a Time

Empower yourself and begin to BUILD confidence!

Building a puzzle takes time, skill, and patience. As each puzzle piece is carefully put into place, the picture begins to emerge. Learning the necessary skills to build confidence is much like building a puzzle. The building process encourages youth, teens, and adults to discover the following:

- ✔ It is important to recognize, admit, and learn from your mistakes.

- ✔ Exiting your comfort zone, welcoming new opportunities, and taking risks will help you to achieve better things and meet your goals.

- ✔ It takes courage to make positive choices and do what is right, even if others criticize you for it.

- ✔ Personal esteem increases as you give your time through service in your community, church, and family.

- ✔ Low self-esteem may prevent forward progression.

- ✔ Self-confident individuals believe in themselves, their abilities to succeed, and live life to its fullest.

- ✔ Happiness is a choice and is available for everyone. Choose to be happy!

Building a "personal" puzzle requires change in perspective, beliefs, and behaviors. Altering thoughts and actions will be challenging. Recognize that change is difficult, and setbacks will occur. In the end, feelings of success and increased self-esteem will be worth the struggles endured through the building process.

Personal Perks

Do you choose to empower yourself? It is important to recognize that your thoughts, words, and actions directly impact your self-esteem. Self-esteem is how you feel about yourself. It's a self-evaluation. In order to answer the question above, it is important to understand the definition of *empower*. To EMPOWER is to give power or authority. POWER is the ability to act or to produce an effect. *Do you choose to* invest power *in yourself each day?*

You have the power to increase your self-esteem and confidence through positive thought patterns and personal perks.

- ✔ Accept yourself for who you are.

- ✔ Know yourself. Recognize and appreciate your strengths. Be willing to improve personal weaknesses.

- ✔ Be at peace with yourself. Are your focus and feelings aligned?

- ✔ Welcome opportunities to be alone. The ability to be alone reflects independence and self-sufficiency.

- ✔ Challenge yourself. Try something new, take up a hobby, or face a fear.

- ✔ Learn to advocate. Speak up and recognize that your opinion counts.

- ✔ Set goals. Identify something you want to accomplish, make a realistic plan and stay focused on your goal.

- ✔ Embrace friends that uplift you. You may need to minimize "toxic" relationships with people who drag you down and decrease your self-worth.

Self-investment is a choice. You are responsible for building your confidence. Make time each day to increase your self-esteem by creating positive patterns that enhance your personal power. Empower yourself through personal perks.

The Bliss List

An action list to empower you!

We live in a world of "lists." A grocery list, a list of errands to run, a list of emails to answer, a list of birthdays to remember, and a list of monthly bills that require payment. An important list that you may be overlooking is the *Bliss List*—an action list that will empower you.

Living an empowered life creates feelings of happiness. Creating your *Bliss List* will help promote feelings of self-worth and joy as you identify your passions, goals, and gratitude. Begin your list by following these six steps:

- ✔ **Your passions.** Ask yourself: What do I love to do? Identify your passions by listing the activities that you enjoy doing or have a desire to do.

- ✔ **Your goals.** List the lifestyle changes that will empower you and increase your confidence. Commit to altering behaviors that will benefit your health, attitude, and relationships and promote increased happiness.

- ✔ **Your gratitude.** Include on your list the people and relationships you are grateful for and why. This will help you identify the relationships in your life that need more of your time and those that do not.

- ✔ **Yourself.** Don't overlook your own accomplishments. Take the time to recognize your successes. Avoid focusing on what you haven't done.

- ✔ **Focus on the obvious.** Keep your list simple and identify the essentials and nonessentials in your life. Essentials are the things you can control and change like your daily exercise routine or your attitude. Nonessentials are those things you cannot control or change like others' happiness or choices. Focus on the essentials and *let go* of the nonessentials.

✔ **Change it up.** Recognize that you can change your list throughout this process. Your *Bliss List* is about self-empowerment and recognizing what makes you happy. There are no correct or incorrect choices.

Consider your choices.

When life offers you a smorgasbord of options, ask yourself: Is this choice supporting my *Bliss List,* and will it empower me and boost my confidence? This will give you clarity between the good choice and the right choice—helping you move towards happiness.

Know Yourself

Is self-esteem learned or inherited? When I ask this question in my seminars most members of the audience answer *inherited.* What do you think?

Self-esteem is learned in our family of origin. It is not inherited. This is great news. If you feel that your self-esteem is low, you have the choice and the power to change it.

Self-esteem is a self-evaluation, and it depends on both one's *personal identity* and one's *social identity. Personal identity* refers to the pride we feel for ourselves based on our personal achievements and accomplishments. *Social identity* refers to the pride we derive from our membership in certain groups, such as families, ethnic groups, occupational groups, neighborhoods, country clubs, and so forth.

If your self-evaluation is positive then your self-esteem is high. Low self-esteem is a negative evaluation of oneself. Is your self-evaluation positive? Take time to evaluate yourself.

Confidence Report

What is a label and why are labels powerful?

A label is a classification. Labels organize us and the world we live in. We label items. We also label ourselves and others. Labels are powerful because we often choose to believe them. Labels affect our self-esteem and our ability to succeed.

As a young girl I was tall, skinny and often called a beanpole. I disliked being told that if I turned sideways and stuck out my tongue I resembled a zipper. My thin appearance and the unkind labels altered my self-esteem because I chose to believe the hurtful messages expressed by my childhood classmates. As an adult, I recognize that those unkind childhood labels no longer define me. I have chosen to replace the negative labels with positive ones.

Can we get rid of negative labels? **YES**, we can.

After one of my seminars a woman spoke with me about a label she had chosen to wear since middle school. A boy in her math class commented on her *stringy, straight* hair, comparing it to her older sister's awesome, great-looking hair.

I asked the woman two questions:

- ✔ "Does your hair define you?" and
- ✔ "Would you like to know how to replace the label?"

Replace labels by following these steps:

- ✔ Be true to yourself by choosing not to believe negative labels if there is no personal benefit. Recognize that there is a difference between constructive criticism and a negative label.

- ✔ Stop reacting to negative impulses.

- ✔ Provide yourself with positive options. Use healthy words to replace the unhealthy words.

✔ Choose to **ACT** and empower yourself.

Avoid negative impulses
Control your thoughts and actions
Turn negatives into positives

We can learn from this quote by Bette Midler, "I didn't belong as a kid, and that always bothered me. If I'd only known that one day my differences would be an asset, then my earlier life would have been much easier."

Are you allowing negative labels to define you?

Redefine Yourself

We choose to label ourselves and others. We "buy into" labels for different reasons. Common labels are smart, attractive, successful, motivated, lazy, rude, shy, and anxious. How many times have you heard others referred to as pushy, aggressive, wimpy, passive, pea-brained, brilliant, gifted or compassionate?

Positive labels increase our self-esteem and negative labels decrease our self-esteem. Believing a label—positive or negative—**is a choice**.

We "buy into" a positive label because it creates a healthy emotional response helping us feel more capable and confident.

With negative labels, we choose to "buy in" because we believe and personalize the label. This is an impulsive response that makes us feel incapable, and we doubt our ability to succeed, which decreases our self-esteem. Decreased self-esteem can paralyze us, and we quit before we get started due to fear of failing.

What labels do you choose to wear?

🧩 Short and Simple

Re-frame your personal labels

Personal labels we *wear* can be changed. First we must choose to change our perception of the word and ourselves. Re-frame negative labels by changing an unhealthy thought to a healthy one.

Change your perception of the behavior in yourself and label the behavior differently—with a healthy, positive word.

Unhealthy label	Healthy label
stubborn	persistent
shy	reserved
hyper	expressive
picky	selective
loud	enthusiastic

Example: I do not see myself as *shy* around my co-workers, just *reserved* when asked to share personal opinions about my work and family.

Reframing personal labels is not meant to excuse inappropriate behavior. It is a strategy to alter negative thought patterns. What unhealthy label will you re-frame?

🧩 A Fresh Start

What results from low self-esteem?

When low self-esteem occurs, an individual may show the following behavior: acting in a self-defeating manner, feeling upset or angry, developing negative thought patterns, and becoming self-absorbed and narrow-minded.

How can you develop skills to raise your self-esteem? *Master empowerment skills and learn to invest power in yourself.*

The following steps will help you raise your self-esteem:

✔ **Make healthy life choices.** Recognize people, relationships, and habits in your life that promote or sustain negative feelings and actions. Remove yourself from those individuals, situations, and habits. Learn to set personal boundaries, and detach from negative thoughts, words, and people.

No one makes you feel badly about yourself unless you allow them. Establish boundaries with your family, friends, and co-workers by voicing your feelings and opinions in reference to criticism. By maintaining personal boundaries with people, you discourage abusive behaviors and empower yourself. You may need to limit your time with certain individuals and detach emotionally. Associate with people who uplift you, and limit your time with those who do not.

✔ **Choose your response.** Don't personalize the incident, avoid impulsive responses, and exercise your power of choice. Stop reacting, and choose to act. Begin by recognizing that you have two choices:

- to be impulsive and overreact, which creates negative feelings, stress, and frustration OR

- to stop, think, and choose a healthy response—one that will result in a positive and effective way

✔ **Identify emotional triggers that promote low self-esteem.** Personal labels are an example of an emotional trigger. Choose to reframe negative thought patterns and labels.

Labels *do* affect our self-esteem. Negative labels promote low self-esteem and positive labels boost our self-esteem. Make healthy life choices, and avoid impulsive responses that create frustration and conflict. A fresh start occurs when you choose to empower yourself by identifying and altering negative labels. Master empowerment and learn to invest in yourself.

Transform Yourself

As you begin to transform yourself you may recognize that change does not happen quickly, and it may be met with some resistance.

Why is change difficult?

Change is difficult because we don't set ourselves up to succeed. Ask yourself these questions?

- ✔ Do I want to take control of my personal choices and actions?
- ✔ Am I making this change for myself or someone else?
- ✔ Do I believe in this change?
- ✔ Do I have a written plan?
- ✔ Is my plan realistic and attainable?

If you answered *no* to any of the above questions, then the next step is to ask yourself, *why?* You will be more successful making life changes if you identify barriers that are holding you back like peer pressure, lack of money or education, or personal fear. These barriers could delay forward progression. It is critical to figure out what's preventing you from making effective change in your life. Understanding and removing barriers is the first step to transforming your life.

The next step is to take charge of change through identifying action steps.

The definition of **change** is *to make different or to alter*. To succeed at change, you must *choose* to succeed.

VISION—*Gain control of your goal by keeping sight of the end result.*

PLAN—*Position yourself for success with action steps and markers.*

BELIEF—*Define "why" change is important and attainable.*

FOCUS—*Maximize positive results by frequently reviewing your plan.*

Transform yourself by making changes to increase your self-esteem. Identify and remove barriers that could delay forward progression. Take action steps and choose to succeed.

Are you ready to make change and are your goals attainable?

Stuck in the Middle

Do you feel stuck in the middle of your life, unable to make change and move forward? Lack of motivation and momentum is frustrating and fosters feelings of failure, decreasing personal self-esteem. Self-investment requires individuals to set goals and outline a plan. Forward progression will not happen by standing still.

Self-investment is similar to puzzle building. Both require action steps. The starting point is where participants feel energetic and determined to succeed. During the puzzle building process, individuals focus on finishing the puzzle, anxious to REAP the benefits of achieving their goal. It is during the middle of the puzzle building process where most people feel overwhelmed and begin to lose focus. Self-investment meets similar frustrations. It is the middle of the process where individuals get bogged down. Building a puzzle and self-investment both require focus, hard work, and motivation.

Let's take a look at four barriers that may decrease your motivation and cause you to get *stuck in the middle* of achieving your goals.

- ✔ **A poor plan.** Is your plan designed for success? Create a plan that is realistic with attainable action steps. If your plan is poorly designed, you will have a loss of vision and momentum.

- ✔ **Mindset.** Is your mindset positive or negative? You will be unable to move forward with your plan if you are feeling negative. Thoughts affect feelings and feelings promote action. If your mindset is not positive, you will not attain your desired goal.

✔ **Loss of momentum.** Are you "spinning your wheels" and unable to move forward? This may cause you to feel too tired to keep going. A lack of knowledge about your goal may be the problem. Step back and re-evaluate the reasons for accomplishing the goal. Be honest with yourself and ensure that the goal is realistic and important to you.

✔ **Lack of accountability.** Hold yourself accountable. Do not blame others or circumstances for set-backs. Everyone needs to be accountable. Accountability promotes feelings of confidence and self-control.

Motivation is required to successfully set and meet goals. Motivation is not a one-time event. It must happen daily. Keep yourself motivated by formulating a solid, attainable plan, and then believe in yourself and your options.

Be aware that motivation has its ups and downs. There are two kinds of motivation: positive and negative. Negative motivation breeds feelings of frustration and exhaustion. Do not choose to degrade yourself and others. Negative thoughts and feelings can dominate your conversations and plan. If this occurs, your self-esteem will deteriorate and forward progression will cease.

Avoid getting *stuck in the middle* of your life by encouraging daily personal growth. Cultivate positive energy and tap into your resources and strengths by recognizing that motivation promotes success. Take the time to invest in yourself by taking action and setting attainable goals.

Pity Party or Power Party

Do you store unwanted clutter in your memory?

Who talks more? According to a study published in *The Journal of Neuroscience*, February 20, 2013, researchers from Maryland University found that women talk more than men. Studies show that the female brain has higher levels of a protein called FOXP2, which is linked with verbal communication. Louann Brizendine, a practicing physician at the University of California-San Francisco and author of *The Female Brain* says that women speak an average of 20,000 words a day vs. 7,000 words for men. We can chalk it up to science—women talk more than men. Keeping this in mind, individuals can choose to have a pity party or a power party by the words and messages they share with themselves and others.

Each day we receive numerous verbal and nonverbal messages about ourselves and our lifestyle. Some of these messages are uplifting and positive and others are not. The negative messages can be absorbed into our minds and hearts lowering our self-esteem. It is important that we learn to be conscious of this process and stop believing the negative messages. Too often we dismiss the positive messages allowing the negative ones to stick on us like post-it notes on a memory board.

We store unwanted clutter in our minds and memory. Mental clutter weighs us down, is frustrating and is a burden. Clutter varies from person to person as does the process of cluttering. Take time each day to de-clutter your mind and heart of unhealthy thoughts and beliefs. Remove the negative post-it notes by following these five steps:

✔ **Attract positives.** Boost your confidence through positive thoughts and actions. Bundle your unhealthy thoughts and behaviors, and discard them. Avoid negative self-talk, and end the negative phrases in your head by replacing them with healthy words. When you think positively, you feel empowered and capable.

✔ **Recognize that affirmations are effective.** An affirmation is a declaration of something that is true. Self-affirmation builds self-esteem and helps us to keep a positive attitude. Make your affirmations personal by using the word 'I'. An example of this is *"I deserve to be happy."*

✔ **Stay optimistic.** Empower yourself through the process of de-cluttering negative thoughts. Empowering yourself from within is a lifestyle change and requires practice. You may have set-backs and experience some ups and downs. Stay optimistic, and be patient with yourself. Avoid looking at set-backs as failures.

✔ **Celebrate small successes.** Take time to recognize the small successes in your day by keeping a gratitude journal or hanging a white board in your office or kitchen and list your daily successes on it—those things you are proud of. Too often we acknowledge only the big successes in ourselves and others. The small "stuff" in our day does count and needs to be recognized. Applaud the simple steps forward in your life and remember whenever a lesson is learned it counts as a success. When we don't recognize each step in the process of making change, we minimize our self-esteem.

✔ **Indulge yourself.** Live a life full of gratitude and service. Be generous with your time and compliments. Allow kind words to uplift you and others. Positive power comes from healthy activities.

Enjoy a power party! Each time you recognize an unhealthy message about yourself, analyze it for accuracy, and replace it with a healthy message. Feeling esteemed and empowered from the inside, will radiate outwardly to others.

Stress Markers

Do demands of the fast-paced world we live in make you feel stressed out? Stress causes headaches, depression, and low self-esteem. Stress is not only bothersome but also extremely unhealthy. Constant pressure can put you at risk.

The most common causes of stress in our society are: money, the economy, relationships, family responsibilities, personal and family health concerns, housing costs, job stability, and personal safety. Which ones affect you?

Stress is not a unitary concept. Stress is multi-faceted. Stress can be defined as the combination of a stressor, stress reactivity, and strain.

A **stressor** is something with the potential to cause a stress reaction. Common stressors come in different forms. Daily hassles create stress, like being stuck in traffic or late for an appointment. Major life events, positive or negative, are also stressors. A job promotion, the birth of a new baby, or the loss of a family member are all major life events that cause a stress reaction.

Life's hassles cause stress, and your response to stressors elicits physiological changes such as increased muscle tension or blood pressure. Physiological changes are **stress reactivity.**

The **strain,** or results of stress reactivity, is physical, psychological or behavioral consequences such as a headache (physical), anxiety (physiological), or aggression (behavioral).

To illustrate that stress is indeed multi-faceted, let's look at a typical stressful day. You're caught in rush hour traffic and are running late for work—this is the stressor. Next, your heart begins to race, and your breathing rate increases. These physiological changes are stress reactivity. Finally, when you arrive at work the strain of the situation causes you to feel frustrated, and you get into an argument with a co-worker over a delayed financial report.

To manage stress effectively in your life, it is important to recognize that there are four major types of stress:

- ✔ **Frustration**—is experienced whenever the pursuit of some goal is thwarted. You feel frustrated when you want something that you cannot have.

- ✔ **Conflict**—occurs when two or more incompatible motivations or behavioral impulses compete for expression.

✔ **Change**—is any noticeable alteration in one's living circumstances that requires adjustment.

✔ **Pressure**—involves expectations or demands that one must behave in a certain way.

Frustration, conflict, change, and pressure cause stress. Stress causes physiological changes to occur like an increased heart rate or muscle tension. To manage such stressors in your life it is critical that you understand yourself and your reactions to stress.

Most of the time, stress is not random, and you are not a passive bystander when it comes to the stress in your life. Too often people create stress for themselves and others. It is important to learn how to buffer yourself from stress. Positive activities, exercise, and healthy behavior are all beneficial to managing daily stress.

Learn to manage stress in your life by following these steps:

✔ Eliminate negative thought patterns.

✔ Speak up and be assertive about your needs and wants.

✔ Recognize your vulnerabilities and strengths.

✔ Increase productivity through exercise and mindfulness meditation.

✔ Understand that empowerment comes from self-knowledge. Increase your knowledge about stress, assessment of stress, and intervention.

Prolonged, chronic stress is unhealthy. Learn to recognize the stress markers in your life, and choose to manage or eliminate them. Stress directly affects your health and wellness. To achieve wellness, the components of your physical, social, mental, spiritual, environmental, and occupational health must be in balance.

Increase your self-esteem and feel more capable by recognizing and managing stress in your life. To help you begin this process, I have created the following Stressed Out questionnaire.

Stressed Out—Questionnaire

It is important to determine what causes you stress, to evaluate your reaction to stress, and to identify ways to minimize stress reactivity.

Major Stressors:

Begin by listing your major stressors. A few examples are: relationships with family, friends or co-workers, finances, academic pressures, or concerns related to personal/professional productivity.

1. _____

2. _____

3. _____

4. _____

Your Reactions:

List the physical, psychological and behavioral reactions that occur when you feel stressed out, for example: increased perspiration, muscle tension, nervousness, anxiety, aggression, withdrawal, denial.

1. _____

2. _____

3. _____

Minimize Stress Reactivity:

List three ways you can minimize the likelihood of stress reactivity when faced with a stressor, for example: to view the situation as less threatening by minimizing negative thoughts and feelings.

1. _____

2. _____

3. _____

Coping:

List three things that you do to manage stress, for example: seeking social support, accountability for your choices, avoidance, or wishful thinking.

1. _____

2. _____

3. _____

Stress Buffers:

Stress buffers are aspects of your life that counterbalance and buffer stress. A few examples are: daily "uplifts" and positive activities like exercise, listening to music, completing a task, or healthy social interactions. List the aspects of your life that seem to buffer stress.

1. _____

2. _____

3. _____

After completing this questionnaire, use the information to prompt healthy responses to daily stressors, helping to minimize stress reactivity and effectively manage stress in your life.

Stress Theory

Is your glass half full or half empty?

Let's get down to business and take a close look at what causes stress. Researchers have established several theories about stress and the negative effects of stress that often result in poor health, disease, and decreased self-esteem. Evidence shows that daily hassles are more harmful to your health than major stressful events. The truth of the matter is, the little things over time add up and cause harmful outcomes to your health and personal wellness.

Stress can result from a variety of stressors—a loss of status, conflict with a family member or friend, threats to self-esteem, work overload, or environmental overcrowding.

Learn to minimize stress by following these three steps:

Uplift yourself. When a situation requires more resources than are available, stress will occur, and your life becomes imbalanced. To manage stress and to create a balanced lifestyle, it is important to provide yourself with daily uplifts. An inspirational thought, a compliment, lunch with a friend or a brisk walk may counteract the daily hassles and help you minimize stress.

Create a buffer. It is important to recognize that attitude affects stress. How you perceive stress is a key component to dealing with stress. If you recognize stress as a challenge and not a threat, less stress will occur. Buffering between stress and the development of illness due to stress is critical. A positive attitude will help decrease stress.

Develop a social network. Many experts recognize that stress occurs when there is not enough social support available. Support comes in a variety of forms such as: emotional support, financial assistance, or physical support. A social network will help you cope with the impact of a stressful event.

Is your glass half full or half empty? An event can be stressful or not—it all depends on your perception of the situation. Take control of the stressors in your life. Your response to stress depends on your resources and coping strategies. Less stress creates a positive lifestyle and increases self-esteem and confidence.

Roadblocks to Stress

Do you control the stress in your life?

Stress is the result of a demand that exceeds your resources to meet that demand. In other words, the demands that you feel are seen as a threat and overwhelming. Each day you experience stressors.

You're running late for work, and you can't find your keys; traffic is slow because of road construction, and when you arrive at your destination you can't find a parking place. Do these scenarios sound familiar? These events lead to stress—the result of the demand exceeding your resources to meet the demand. What can you do to cope with stress?

Coping is to engage in thoughts or behaviors as a response to stress, establishing strategies to help manage everyday stressors like those mentioned above. Stress begins with a life situation that knocks you out of balance. Coping strategies help bring you back to balance after being nudged or shoved into disequilibrium caused by an argument with another person, the death of a loved one, or some other change in your life that requires you to adapt.

Intervention involves activities that prevent a stressor from producing negative consequences. Setting up roadblocks is the key to intervention. Roadblocks may include: positive thought patterns, meditation, exercise, or a brisk walk. Setting up roadblocks between the life situation and your perception of the situation is the first step. Take the time to look at the situation realistically, not emotionally. Emotions drive feelings of fear, anxiety, and self-doubt. For example, you receive an evaluation at work that does not meet your expectations. Your immediate reaction may be distressing because you fear being fired. This is a normal response but not a healthy response. Set up roadblocks and prevent this stressor from paralyzing you.

Self-talk is a technique that requires some objectivity. Talk yourself through the situation. Be objective and realistic—not emotional.

Example: *This evaluation is helpful. This is an opportunity for me to adjust my thinking and behavior to meet the objectives set my employer.*

Re-label negative concepts of yourself and the situation. Focus on the positives, not the negatives.

Example: *I am not a failure at my current job. I recognize ways to improve my work performance. I will work on the following...*

Thought stopping is to shut off negative thoughts. Refuse to let negative thoughts continue by controlling your thought patterns. Replace negative thought patterns with a positive action step.

Example: *I will not focus on the possibility of being fired. I will focus on improving my performance.*

Environmental planning is also a helpful way to create roadblocks to stress. Evaluate your environment to avoid anxiety-provoking stimulus.

Example: *Distractions prevent me from focusing on the important aspects of my job and decrease my productivity. I will set time aside each day to review emails and correspondence.*

Resiliency is the ability to make use of your strengths and assets in regard to challenges. Individuals can be taught certain qualities that will help them rise above challenges and adversity. Resilient qualities include optimism, happiness, self-determination, creativity, sense of morality and self-control, gratitude, forgiveness, and humility. Identify your strengths and skills. Life's challenges can be positive experiences when viewed as opportunities to learn and grow.

Many people find coping techniques difficult to embrace and practice. A critical step to coping is to understand selective awareness. Selective awareness is making the decision to focus on the good or the bad in a stressful situation. When you are faced with a stress situation ask yourself, "Am I seeing the glass half full or half empty?"

Managing stress is simply exercising your ability to take control of your choices and actions. You are in charge of your behavior. Changing others' behavior may not be an option, but you can control how you react to their behavior. You have more control over yourself and daily stressors than you may think. Taking charge of yourself and the roadblocks to stress increases self-esteem and builds confidence.

🧩 Smart Choice

Do you practice constructive strategies when coping with stress?

Stress is often seen as an overwhelming, traumatic crisis like a terrorist attack or a devastating hurricane. Major disasters are extremely stressful, however these unusual events are a small part of what causes stress; everyday events like losing your car keys, waiting in a long line at the bank, or having a disagreement with your spouse are also stressful.

It is important to recognize that a minor stress can create major effects. Research shows that everyday hassles may have harmful effects on mental and physical health. Unfortunately, chronic stress leads to poor health. To avoid chronic stress it is critical to manage daily stressors. Stress researchers recommend that individuals learn coping skills, recognize their own limitations, and take time to relax.

People perceive stress and react to it very differently. The appraisal of stress lies in the eye and the mind of the beholder. Situations that cause stress for one person may not cause stress for another. Some people tend to react to stressors in such a way that it takes a toll on their overall health. In other words their bodies over-react to stressful situations. In these cases, it is extremely important to learn and use stress management techniques. Approximately half of all deaths in the United States are caused by poor health, a lack of physical exercise, smoking and the inability to manage stress.

Stress happens when circumstances threaten or are perceived to threaten your well-being or tax your coping abilities. Psychologist and University of California, Berkeley professor, Richard Lazarus, explains stress to be the result of a determination that exceeds resources available to meet that demand. Coping is to engage in a behavior or thought in response to the demands of stress.

The human response to stress is multidimensional, and people cope with stress in different ways. Coping with stress can be challenging because stress is created by a variety of situations. There are two approaches to coping with stress—defensive coping or constructive coping.

Defensive coping occurs when defense mechanisms shield an individual from the emotional discomfort of stress through self-deception. This deception involves mechanisms that protect a person from unpleasant emotions such as anxiety and guilt. Distorting reality so it does not seem so threatening operates at varying levels of awareness, although they are largely unconscious. This behavior is generally less than optimal because avoidance rarely solves problems.

Defensive coping is an unhealthy, negative approach to stress and promotes the following behaviors:

To give up. Many people simply give up and withdraw when faced with daily stressors. This passive behavior is also referred to as *learned helplessness* and occurs when individuals believe that events and situations are beyond their control. Researchers have found that this coping pattern is associated with increased rather than decreased distress. It is important to note that in certain circumstances it may make sense for an individual to disengage when they struggle to pursue a goal that turns out to be unattainable.

To blame oneself. This is another common response to stress and difficulties. Many influential theorists have recognized the tendency to become highly self-critical in response to stress. American psychologist, Albert Ellis, referred to this phenomenon as *"catastrophic thinking"* recognizing that the behavior causes, aggravates, and perpetuates emotional reactions to stress that can be problematic. It is important to recognize personal weaknesses and failures but excessive self-blame is extremely unhealthy.

To lash out at others. Aggression is any behavior that is intended to hurt someone, either verbally or physically. Lashing out involves aggressive behavior due to frustration that generally creates additional stress. Books, magazines, and numerous self-help articles advise that it is healthy to reduce anger by "blowing off steam." However, most experimental research finds that behaving in an aggressive manner tends to fuel more anger and aggression. Better results come from other behaviors such as talking or writing about one's problems, frustrations, and emotions.

To indulge oneself. Impulsive and self-indulgence behaviors result in excessive and unwise patterns of eating, drinking, smoking, drug use, spending money, or Internet use. Studies have linked stress to such behaviors.

Constructive coping takes place when you engage in a behavior or thought to respond to the demands of stress. Altering your appraisal of stress is a healthy, positive approach to managing daily stressors. Positive coping tactics include the following:

- ✔ It is essential to confront your problems directly.

- ✔ You must base your thinking on a realistic appraisal of your stress and coping resources. Avoid self-deception and negative, unrealistic thinking. Irrational assumptions about stress may promote unrealistic appraisals, resulting in unhealthy behaviors.

- ✔ Learn to recognize, and in some cases, inhibit negative emotional reactions to stress.

- ✔ Make efforts to ensure that your body and health are not vulnerable to the damaging effects of stress.

Learning to cope with stress is critical to maintaining good health. Numerous examples of the relationship between stress and poor health are available for review in today's world. Historical trends in the death rate for contagious diseases such as measles, whooping cough, and scarlet fever has declined as a threat to our health. However, the death rate for stress-related chronic diseases like heart disease, cancer, and stroke has remained quite high.

Take time to invest in your health by learning to cope with stress. Three factors that influence stress are: social support, optimism, and an awareness of the individual differences in how people tolerate stress. Implementing strategies to manage and reduce daily stressors in your life is a smart choice. Begin today!

The Winning Equation

Decreased Stress = Increased Productivity

Is life handing you "stuff"—that makes you feel stressed? The truth is the bills will keep coming, there will never be enough time in the day, and keeping up with family and work will always be a juggling act. The answer lies in your ability to manage the "stuff" in your life. You can choose to take control of your life or let the "stuff" control you.

Technology may be a source of your stress. It allows us to do more, but it may also cause you to feel overwhelmed and distracted. Technostress is your reaction to technology and how your life is changing as a result of cell phones, computers and email. Research tells us that technology causes five hours of stress per week. Taking control of your life is the foundation of stress management.

These three steps will be helpful as you choose to manage stress:

1. **Identify the source of stress.**

   • Look at your habits, attitudes, and behavior and identify the source of your stress.

   • Assess how you feel, both physically and emotionally, during stressful times in your life.

   • After identifying common stressors, take a close look at how you think, feel, and act in response to stress.

2. **Cope with stress.**

   • Look at how you manage stress in your daily routine.

- Are your coping strategies healthy, productive, and are they working?
- Eliminate unhealthy and non-productive strategies to coping with stress, and replace them with positive strategies.

3. **Reinforce positive strategies that help reduce stress.**
   - Learn to say "no."
   - Manage your time and to-do list more effectively.
   - Be more assertive, and learn to self-advocate.
   - Avoid negative people who drag you down and cause you stress.
   - Adapt and be willing to compromise.
   - Recognize that a goal to master perfection is not realistic.

Reduce stressors by replacing negative emotions with positive emotions. Positive emotions will alter your mindset, broaden your scope of attention, and increase your productivity and flexibility to problem-solve.

Positive emotions can also undo the lingering effects of negative emotions and short-circuit potentially damaging physiological responses to stress. Research shows that mind/body programs, relaxation techniques, and problem-solving strategies lead to less depression and less cognitive decline.

Finally, positive emotions can promote rewarding social interactions that help build valuable social support, enhance coping strategies and other enduring personal resources.

Learning to decrease stress in your life will increase your personal productivity and help you gain control of the "stuff" in your world instead of letting the "stuff" control you.

🧩 Punch List

Resolve stress by managing your behavior

Life-situations and interpersonal relationships may cause stress. The first step to reducing stress in your life that occurs from such stressors is to learn effective ways to manage your own behavior.

Use effective communication. It is important when communicating with others that you make your feelings known. You have the right to speak up and advocate for yourself. Effective communication skills will help you get along better with people you interact with, and it will also reduce stress.

There are two types of communication: nonverbal and verbal. **Nonverbal communication** is our body language—posture, hand gestures, and facial expressions. Body language is physical behavior, and it allows you to communicate to others without saying one word. A friendly smile is a nonverbal communication that says "hello" to a stranger in any language. Scratching our heads expresses feelings of confusion, and a hug is an expression of love and acceptance. We all recognize the importance of communicating nonverbally; however, you need to recognize that nonverbal communication of feelings and thoughts can be easily misinterpreted. **Verbal communication** is expressed through language and the use of words. It is critical that nonverbal and verbal messages are as consistent as possible.

The following ideas will help you be an effective communicator:

- ✔ Plan time to talk and allow sufficient time to have meaningful discussions.
- ✔ Eliminate distractions by turning off your cell phone and the television.

✔ Be honest when expressing your feelings. This may seem risky, but it is important to share your feelings and not expect the other person to guess what they are.

✔ Be accountable for your thoughts and actions during the conversation. Think before you speak.

✔ Approach the conversation by clarifying the goals of the discussion and what behaviors need to be altered and improved.

✔ Be an active listener. Paraphrase the speaker's words to make certain that you understand their thoughts and feelings.

✔ Begin the discussion with what you agree on—not what you disagree on. When you open the conversation with the points you agree on, your discussion gets off to a positive start. If you are discussing finances with your spouse, you might begin by saying, "I agree that it is important that we establish a workable monthly budget." This begins the conversation with a point of agreement.

✔ Avoid using the word "but." The word "but" erases everything that precedes it. When someone says, "Yes, your opinion is important, but…" they are really saying, "Your opinion may be important, but my opinion is more important." Use the word "and" instead of "but" and let others know that you are listening to them. "And" says to others, your needs are important and I am willing to consider your point of view.

✔ Use "I" statements when communicating your feelings and viewpoint. "I" statements place focus on your behavior and not on others. If you are responding to a request made by your boss to work more hours use the word "I." For example, you might say, "When I am asked to work additional hours, I feel frustrated and overwhelmed." Avoid saying to your boss, "When you ask me to work more hours, it makes me feel frustrated and overwhelmed." Try not to place focus on others' behavior when making direct requests.

✔ Refrain from using "why" questions. They tend to make others feel defensive. Avoid asking your spouse, "Why don't you spend more time with me?" Instead, rephrase the question to a statement: "I feel that we don't spend enough time together."

Emotional intelligence prevents and resolves conflict. Emotional intelligence is the ability to accurately identify and understand your own emotional reactions and the emotions of others.

Author and psychologist, Daniel Goleman, was the first person to define and popularize emotional intelligence. His model of emotional intelligence has been condensed into the four branch model:

✔ Accurately perceive emotions in yourself and others.
✔ Use emotions to facilitate thinking.
✔ Understand emotional meaning.
✔ Manage emotions.

To develop and maintain healthy relationships, it is important to understand emotional intelligence. Without emotional intelligence, you will not be cognizant of your own feelings and others' feelings, which are important to human interpretation and interaction.

Exercise control of your time to reduce stress. Managing personal time is often a challenge. Effective management techniques include the following:

✔ Evaluate how you spend your time. You cannot change what you aren't aware of.

✔ Set goals to improve your time management: daily, weekly, monthly, yearly, and long-range.

✔ Prioritize your goals once you have identified them. Not all of your goals will be of equal importance. Maximize the chances of achieving your goals by organizing them from most important to least important.

✔ Make a list of things *not* to do. If you tend to waste time playing computer games, include this activity on your not-to-do list.

✔ Schedule your time by listing the most important tasks first. Be realistic about what you can accomplish in a day, and remember to schedule time for you.

✔ Maximize your rewards by organizing your time. Make sure that you identify and engage in activities that create forward progression, build confidence, and provide rewards.

✔ Learn to say *no*. Do not say *yes*, when you want to say *no*. This will create feelings of frustration and resentment.

✔ Delegate tasks that do not need your personal attention. Do not hesitate to ask for help when you feel overwhelmed, overloaded, or short on time. This does not mean that you will use other people to do your work. In return, help others when they need help, and you have available time.

✔ Schedule time for interruptions. It is impossible to eliminate all day-to-day interruptions, so plan time in your schedule to deal with them.

Social networks help to buffer stressors. Social support is belonging, being accepted, and feeling loved or needed. Research shows that social interaction and supporting others is beneficial to your health.

Learn to manage and eliminate daily stress by doing the following:

✔ Resolve conflict by being an active listener and exploring alternate solutions to the problem.

✔ Improve your communications skills by making certain that your nonverbal and verbal messages are consistent.

✔ Review your time management skills and make adjustments when necessary.

✔ Recognize the health benefits of a strong social network.

What lifestyle change will you make to minimize personal stress? Take action and resolve stress by learning to manage your own behavior. Effective communication, accurately identifying and understanding your own emotional reactions, managing your time, and creating a positive social network will help you minimize daily stress in your life, and feel increased happiness.

Celebrate Stress!

Most people view stress as unhealthy due to the negative emotional responses brought on by stress, that include annoyance, anger, anxiety, fear, sadness, and grief. Stress can be defined as any circumstance that threatens one's well-being. Stress may also be viewed as the difference between pressure and adaptability.

The human response to stress is complex, and when under stress, people often react emotionally. Recently researchers have uncovered some strong links between specific cognitive reactions to stress and specific emotions. For example, self-blame may lead to guilt, and helplessness may cause feelings of sadness.

Many daily stresses seem to come and go without leaving long-term consequences, however, a variety of negative emotions can accompany stressful situations. The emotions felt by U.S. citizens after the devastation of 9/11 included anger, sadness, and fear. However, along with negative feelings, positive emotions also emerged. People expressed feelings of gratitude for the safety of their family, and many expressed love for their family, friends, and country. Positive emotions appear to help people rebound from stress.

Research tends to focus on the connection between stress and negative emotions, but it is important to note that positive emotions also occur during times of stress. In recent years, studies have focused on four positive effects of stress:

✔ **Personal growth and self-improvement.** Studies on resilience suggest that stress can promote personal growth and self-improvement. Resiliency is the ability to identify, and utilize strengths and assets to respond to challenges.

My neighbor's husband lost his job because his company downsized. This was an extremely stressful time for the entire family, and because of their circumstances the older children got part-time jobs working at local businesses. After several months of interviewing, her husband found a new job. She told me that the job loss was initially devastating, but the outcome was extremely positive. It caused her family to pull together, work together, and grow together. Her children learned the importance of utilizing personal resources in an effort to manage stress.

✔ **Re-evaluate priorities.** Stressful situations can encourage people to gain new insights and re-evaluate their priorities.

A good friend of mine shifted her priorities when her mother was diagnosed with cancer. The circumstances caused her to take on additional tasks like driving her mom to radiation treatments, doctor appointments and attending to her daily needs. This situation prompted my friend to re-evaluate her priorities. Through the process of caring for her mom, she gained new insights about herself, and her ability to focus on the *essentials* in life, and to let go of the *nonessentials*.

✔ **Opportunities to learn new skills.** Adapting to stress may lead to personal changes that are changes for the best. Through change, new strengths and skills may be acquired.

Over the years, our family has moved several times. With each job promotion we found ourselves packing up, and relocating to a different state. Finding a new home, getting our boys settled in new schools, and establishing my career in a new city was challenging. These changes caused stress, but I acquired new skills because of these challenges. I learned to network, advocate for myself and our children, and to be adaptable.

✔ **Ability to cope.** Confronting and conquering a stressful situation may lead to improvements in coping abilities thus increasing one's self-concept and confidence.

Years ago my son came home from grade school upset because he got a poor grade on his math exam. My first instinct was to react, and yell at him for his poor performance on the test. A better approach was to calmly talk to him about what he could do moving forward to improve his grade, and study skills. Healthy coping strategies were required to help me, and my son manage the stress of the situation. I knew my son would feel more confident taking his next test if he made positive changes in his approach to learning the material.

Stress is part of life, and people deal with it every day. Take the time to celebrate stress. Recognize that courage, perseverance, and resilience are human strengths that can promote positive effects of stress.

> *We want to be more successful, but that means*
> *we must also recharge and renew ourselves.*
> *Stress becomes toxic when it accumulates.*
> —*Arianna Huffington*

Mind Body Motivation

Are you feeling sluggish, anxious, and stressed out? The remedy can be simple—**exercise!** Research tells us that exercise brings a more satisfied lifestyle. Researchers from Penn State University found that people's daily physical activity is directly related to satisfaction with life.

David Conroy, professor of kinesiology at the university said, "Shifts in depression, anxiety and stress would be expected to influence a person's satisfaction with life at any given point in time. In addition, fatigue can be a barrier to engaging in physical activity, and a high Body Mass Index associated with being overweight may cause a person to be less satisfied in a variety of ways."

"We found that people's satisfaction with life was directly impacted by their daily physical activity," said Jaclyn Maher, Penn State graduate student in kinesiology. Based on their findings, the researchers confirmed a greater amount of physical activity can positively improve satisfaction with life.

Empower yourself daily through exercise. The first step is to get started. Run on the tread mill, join an aerobics class at the local gym, or take a brisk walk during your lunch break. The key to feeling less stress and increased self-esteem is to start moving and to exercise!

To stay motivated it is important to remove barriers and be aware of situations or thoughts that may generate a negative outcome and prevent you from succeeding. Barriers will drain your energy physically and emotionally, perpetuating additional stress and feelings of failure. After removing barriers the next step is to find solutions that will help you move forward.

Common barriers and solutions are:

- ✔ **Negatives.** Negative thoughts about exercise will prevent momentum. If a temporary setback occurs, take the time to re-evaluate your game plan and make adjustments.

   Solution: Believe in yourself and the benefits that daily exercise can provide.

- ✔ **Defensiveness.** Change is difficult. Breaking old habits and starting new ones is a challenge. Do not be overly critical of yourself when minor setbacks occur. Feel secure about yourself, and be open to ideas to improve your plan.

   Solution: The buddy system may be the key to keeping you motivated. Ask your friends and family for their support.

Run with a friend or join the aerobics class your sister is enrolled in. Feel secure about yourself, and be open to ideas to improve your plan.

✔ **Bullying.** Do not bully yourself by putting yourself down if success is not met immediately. Remember change takes time.

Solution: Focus on the positive by keeping a journal about your progress, and highlight the positives. Do not dismiss your accomplishments, and take the time to applaud your successes.

✔ **A lack of accountability.** Make certain your goal is attainable and measurable. It is important to be accountable for the outcome of your effort.

Solution: Find ways to make your plan work, and do not give up.

✔ **Limited belief.** Negative thoughts about yourself and your progress will prevent success from occurring. Demeaning thoughts will only make the process more difficult.

Solution: To remain motivated and positive place inspiring notes and quotes on your door or mirror. Review these thoughts prior to exercising. Listen to upbeat music while exercising, and be inspired!

Get out of the dumps and empower yourself through exercise. Shift your unhealthy feelings of anxiety and stress to healthy feelings of self-esteem and confidence by engaging in daily physical activity. Avoid barriers that may prevent forward progression by setting yourself up for success.

Boost Your Confidence—Choose to Forgive

Forgiveness is difficult. Forgiving yourself and others for past mistakes is a hard step to take and one that requires humility. Pride prevents the process of forgiveness from happening.

Forgiveness begins with a change of heart and perspective. First, you must feel forgiveness in your heart, and then you will have the insight and strength to alter your viewpoint about the situation.

Pardoning someone who has hurt you, whether deliberately or unintentionally, is really more about you than them. It is impossible to change others, and it is not your responsibility to try. You are only responsible for your own thoughts and actions. Trying to change the person who has hurt you is a waste of energy and time. Spend time changing your own heart and mindset.

If you choose not to forgive, you will continue to feel helpless, frustrated, and trapped by anger. The inability to forgive will rob you of your power.

Forgiveness will give you renewed feelings of energy and joy. You will be free of anger, remorse, and guilt. Boost your confidence and empower yourself. Choose to forgive.

Discover Yourself and THRIVE

What prevents you from thriving? It may be a lack of clarity of what you need and want. These circumstances and state of mind will prevent thriving conditions for you and decrease your self-esteem.

Discover YOU by answering this important question: How do I define myself?

You will thrive when your self-definition and the direction your life is moving in are compatible.

Limitations also prevent forward progression and the ability to thrive. Personal limitations are habits, situations, beliefs, or handicaps that prevent forward progression.

It is important that you recognize the difference between *manageable* and *changeable* limitations.

Manageable limitations are limitations that you do not have the ability to alter, such as physical, emotional, or mental handicaps.

Changeable limitations are limitations that you have the power to alter, such as procrastination, negative self-talk, or an unhealthy lifestyle.

An example of altering a changeable limitation is a grandmother who wants to communicate with her grandchildren (who live in another state) through email. A lack of computer knowledge prevents her from accomplishing this task. To change this limitation she registers for an *Intro to Computers* class at the local community college.

Embrace Self-Induced Limitations and THRIVE

Recognize that you can change self-induced limitations. Three common self-induced limitations are:

Fear of Failure

Lack of Self Control

Transfer of Blame

  ✔ *Fear of Failure*—being afraid to try something new or to make change

  Example: Your neighbor has a beautiful singing voice, but she refuses to try out for the community musical because she is convinced that she won't perform well at the tryout. Her fear is immobilizing, and she does not try out.

Lesson: It is critical to understand that fear is an obstacle to personal growth and progression only if we allow it to be. To move past fear of failing—recognize that when you try something new, you risk failure.

✔ *Lack of Self Control*—absence of balance in personal choices

Example: Your co-worker notices that she has gained some unwanted pounds and invites you to walk with her for thirty minutes during your lunch hour. Within two weeks she finds excuses not to walk and decides that losing weight is too difficult.

Lesson: Self-discipline is the key! It is also important to believe in the goal, have a realistic plan, and stay focused.

✔ *Transfer of Blame*—not willing to take responsibility for the consequences of personal choices

Example: Your daughter never takes responsibility for her choice to procrastinate. When her homework and house-hold chores are not done she finds excuses for her behavior and blames others for her poor use of time.

Lesson: It is important to teach her this lesson: If you don't own it, you can't change it!

Choose to Thrive! THRIVE by recognizing who you are and moving your life in a direction that is compatible with your self-definition. Do not allow limitations to hold you back!

Go All-Out! Live Life with a Purpose

Living life with a purpose is a choice and is one of the most self-actualized activities we can participate in. Unfortunately, some individuals choose to remain mediocre, never recognizing their full potential or purpose.

A self-actualized person is one who has an exceptionally healthy personality and is engaged in continual personal growth. Psychologist, Abraham Maslow, argued that human nature should be viewed from an optimistic viewpoint rather than dwelling on human disorder and dysfunction.

To live a life with purpose, it is important to be a self-actualizer, one who is accurately tuned into reality, enjoys rewarding interpersonal relationships, and is at peace with oneself. Optimally, you should feel happy and fulfilled, most of the time. We all have a few bad days, when happiness and fulfillment may elude us. The point is, when you review your life, have you experienced more joy and contentment than disappointment and unhappiness? Your moments of satisfaction, excitement, and happiness should outnumber your feelings of frustration, guilt, and boredom.

Begin this process by analyzing your focus and feelings—are they compatible and balanced? Feelings of contentment, joy and clarity occur when your focus and feelings are aligned.

The following steps will help you identify your purpose and potential:

✔ **Listen**—*Most of the successful people I've known are the ones who do more listening than talking.*—Bernard M. Baruch

Life has a way of showing you your purpose—if you take the time to listen. Listen to your heart and identify what you love to do. It is also important to listen to others and gain insights from their wisdom and life experiences. Listening is a necessary step to personal growth and improvement.

✔ **Learn**—*Change is the end result of all true learning.* —Leo Buscaglia

Increased knowledge and understanding is a key component to personal growth and satisfaction. A healthy self-concept is enhanced through learning.

✔ **Live**—*I think my mother… made it clear that you have to live life by your own terms and you have to not worry about what other people think and you have to have the courage to do the unexpected.*—Caroline Kennedy

Appreciate opportunities to live life and have "peak experiences" often. Utilize your talents, pursue your interests, and recognize your contributions. Take advantage of life experiences that force you to move "out of your comfort zone" and view life from a different perspective.

✔ **Labor**—*The dictionary is the only place that success comes before work. Work is the key to success, and hard work can help you accomplish anything.*—Vince Lombardi Jr.

To labor is to work. Labor is defined as physical or mental exertion, doing a specific task. How do you feel about your work, do you find it exciting and satisfying? If not, brainstorm ways to find new directions and passions. If the work you do is not satisfying or exciting, it may be time to make a career change or alter your mindset about the work you do each day. Hard work is a strong predictor of happiness. To feel happy, take action, roll up your sleeves, and engage in work.

✔ **Love**—*Don't aim for success if you want it; just do what you love and believe in, and it will come naturally.*—David Frost

Love what you do, and do what you love. Make time in your busy schedule to develop a strong social network. Nurture feelings of kinship with family and friends. Enjoy a sense of belonging, and recognize the need for love and healthy relationships in your daily routine.

✔ **Laugh**—*The most wasted of all days is one without laughter.*—E.E. Cummings

Enjoy your sense of humor, and invite laughter into your life. Recognize that laughter promotes feelings of spontaneity and, naturalness and fosters feelings of independence.

Learn to laugh at yourself. Laughter can lessen feelings of despair, resentment, and failure.

Choose to Listen, Learn, Live, Labor, Love and Laugh.

Indulge yourself through involvement in healthy activities. Serve in your family, church, and community. Giving to others will help you live life with purpose.

Cultivate a culture of cooperation. It is difficult to find purpose in life while simultaneously dragging others down through criticism and control. Cooperation promotes social connectedness and evokes gratitude and kindness in yourself and others.

Kindness is not always easy. Start with yourself. Recognize and appreciate your strengths and talents. Elevate yourself and others through compliments and positive collaboration.

Happiness leads to success because it promotes better thinking and problem-solving skills, and increases motivation, creativity and energy. Recognizing your purpose and reaching your potential heightens your self-concept and increases personal joy.

Go all-out and live life with a purpose by appreciating and acknowledging others contributions. Your happiness will be heightened by elevating those around you. Reaching your potential will be the end-result of your ability to compromise, compliment and love yourself and those around you.

Be on the A-list

I have been given permission to print my friend's blog post. It demonstrates how altering self-perceptions can empower and build confidence.

Before I start sharing my "new and interesting" ideas, I want to write about what has made the great change in me. I have gotten a lot of comments on how much I have changed in the recent months. There is a good reason for this.

I recently moved and am in the process of getting a divorce. The first thing I did was go to counseling. Some look down on this, but there was no way I was going to let this situation scar me the way I have seen it do to so many others. While talking in one of my sessions I mentioned that there was a guy I know that I wouldn't mind going on a date with after my divorce, but I said that *"he was way out of my league."* Of course this statement was chalked up to bad self-esteem.

I went home and talked to my mom about my session. She said something so simple, but little did she know that it would make such an impact. "Jessie, you put yourself on the B-list a long time ago." WOW! It hit me like a ton of bricks! I don't know if it was just the right time or phrased the right way, but from that second on, I viewed myself differently.

What my mom said was true. I had put myself on the B-list a long time ago and put others above me. Whether it was because I was stuck on past mistakes or because I didn't feel as pretty as the others girls, I am not sure. But I am sure that my life has been changed since I made the decision to put myself back on the A-list.

At first I felt like I was playing a role. I walked with my head held high and shoulders back. I talked to people that I never had the courage to talk with before. It was amazing how soon it didn't feel like an act anymore. Soon it was just me!! So if you see a change in me—that is why. I put myself back on the A-list.

I believe that we are all sent here on the A-list. Somewhere along the way we let others or ourselves make us feel like we are less than our best. But we can get it back. It can change our lives.

Build Your Brilliance

One of my favorite Broadway songs is **Diamonds Are a Girl's Best Friend,** which was introduced by Carol Channing in the original Broadway production of *Gentlemen Prefer Blondes* (1953).

Like each of you, no two diamonds are alike. Every diamond is a miracle of time. The formation of a natural diamond under the Earth's crust can be anywhere from under 1 billion years to more than 3.3 billion years. Building your personal brilliance is similar to the formation of a natural diamond; it takes time and is a life-long process.

The word diamond comes from the Greek word "adamas," meaning indestructible. Building confidence helps you to become strong and indestructible when faced with challenges, daily hassles and life altering events. It helps you to be resilient and capable of accessing your strengths and assets when managing stress.

Brilliance is defined as great brightness; radiance, excellence, or exceptional talent. Like the definition, you can discover your brilliance.

1. The first step to building personal brilliance and increasing confidence is to accept change as a constant in life. Altering negative behaviors creates the opportunity for excellence and personal growth. Most of life's significant lessons are learned through change. Allow change to empower you by viewing it as freedom—not fear. Change may force you out of your comfort zone, but it provides you an opportunity to stretch yourself. When you make positive lifestyle change you become stronger and more brilliant.

2. The development of self-efficacy is the next step to building brilliance. Self-efficacy is having confidence in your ability to perform and effectively carry out change. It is a predictor of success.

3. Accountability for your actions is the third step. With every thought and action there are consequences. Learning to accept the consequences of your behavior builds confidence, brightness and increases personal self-esteem.

4. The fourth step is to live well and be healthy. Managing stress, eating healthy foods, exercising and getting enough

sleep top the list of strategies for living well. You perform better at daily tasks if you are healthy. Put minor stressors into perspective, focus on the positive aspects of your life, self-monitor your behavior in regards to exercise, healthy eating habits, and if necessary, improve your sleep routine.

5. The fifth step to building your brilliance is to appraise your perceptions daily. Perceptions are the cognitive interpretations of people, things and events in your world. Choose to focus on the positives rather than the negatives. Be your own best friend. Recognize that you control more than you may think. Do not spend your time controlling others; it is a waste of time and energy. Strike a balance; you are neither in complete control of everything, nor are you without any control.

You are what you think. Radiate excellence by increasing your confidence, accepting change as a constant in your life, developing self-efficacy, being accountable for your actions, and keeping minor stressors in perspective. Appraise your perceptions every day and focus on the positives in the world around you. See yourself as brilliant and confident.

Whatever you want in life, other people are going to want it too. Believe in yourself enough to accept the idea that you have an equal right to it.
Diane Sawyer

BElieve in YOUrself!

Boost your self-esteem

Education is essential

Learn tolerance

Invest in your abilities

Elevate your thoughts and actions

Victories are earned not given

Enjoy the journey

Feel Capable

If you plan on being anything less than you are capable of being, you will probably be unhappy all the days of your life.

-Abraham Maslow

PUZZLE PIECES IN THIS SECTION:

If I Play by the Rules, Do I Win?

Growing up I was taught numerous rules by my parents and teachers. Rules and guidelines keep us safe, teach us to be polite, and help us to navigate our way through life. Without rules there is chaos. Rules establish order and are necessary for personal growth and increased self-esteem.

During childhood, I learned three rules: honesty is the best policy; you can't always have what you want; and the highest score wins. Throughout the years, my perspective on these rules has changed.

First, let's look at the definition of perspective. Perspective is defined as your point of view or the choice of context for opinions, beliefs, and experiences. In other words, it's your idea or viewpoint about something based on your opinions, beliefs, and experiences. As an adult, my perspective is different about these three rules, because my opinions, beliefs, and experiences have changed over the years.

Now, let's take a closer look at these so-called rules I was taught as a child and my perspective on them today.

Honesty is the best policy. Be honest with yourself about your feelings, needs and motives. Often we put ourselves on the "back burner" while we tend to everyone else's needs. This is not wise or healthy. Take time for you, recognize that your feelings are important, and learn to advocate for yourself. Speak up for what you want and what is important to you. The bottom line is, you must be honest with yourself before you can be honest with others. Honesty is the best policy.

You can't always have what you want. Why not? In a lot of ways you can, but clarity is the key. Be clear about what you want and how you can attain it. Create a plan that is attainable, works for you and does not compromise your integrity. *Remember—timing is everything.* Perhaps you can't have it all right now, but you can have what you want if your goal is realistic, and you are willing to work for it. Hard work is a strong predictor of happiness. So go for it!

The highest score wins. It depends on the game you are playing. If you are a fan of tennis or basketball then yes, high score wins. If golf is your game then no, high score does not win. Playing the game is more important than winning the game. Change your perspective about winning in life. It's not about the competition. Be grateful for the opportunity to be a participant. Staying in the race is the key. Crossing the finish line first does not always make you the winner.

If I play by the rules, do I win? Yes, if you are playing the correct game. Life offers us a smorgasbord of positive options. Deciding which choice is right for you at specific times in your life might be the challenge. Avoid being impulsive or emotional when it comes to making decisions. Look at all possible options and go with the right choice not the good choice. If that choice proves to be wrong, it's okay to choose again. Do not look at incorrect choices as failures. Recognize and value the importance of rules. They are part of life's process and necessary to personal growth and success.

The Race

By: Debbe Collett

Speed doesn't matter, nor does the pace
For this is a very unusual race.
We'll all have a time before reaching its end
That will require of us our hand to lend.
Time won't determine or make us a star,
But time well spent will be better by far.
Our speed in this race won't help us at all,
But what we do is what will make us stand tall.
No banners or bands will greet us alone,
But music so grand will surround the throne.
There may be a time we must lead a small pack

And carefully keep them on the right track
Or for a time we may go and gather lost sheep
To bring back to the race and their pace to keep.
We'll lift up the fallen; we'll lend a hand
Love is there for every man.
We'll all require at a point in this race
Acceptance, forgiveness, a loving embrace,
There may be a day it is us who is standing there
Alone with a burden, needing someone to care,
With heavy hearts having lost sight of the light
Then we'll need that someone to come back in the night.
They'll just take our hand, say come follow my stride
And we'll know there. Right there by our side,
Our hearts will feel humbled, but together we'll go
Back to that race we knew long ago.
It's hope that will then become our best friend
And with hard work and faith we'll move forward again.
We all only want to finish this race home,
But true joy won't be felt if we come in alone.
That's why we all need to help one another.
We must go back to look for each other,
For if we lose sight, or leave one behind,
Such sorrow we'll find at the finish line.
So the value of keeping the very best pace
Won't help you win in this glorious race.

Comfort Zone

Do you take time to nurture yourself?

External demands can over-power our lives. Too often our schedules are managed and controlled by others, and we neglect to take time each day to recognize and value ourselves.

Strengthening the "inner core" is not just about engaging in exercise for your mid-section. It is about strengthening the inner-self, the soul of you. How do you show love and appreciation for yourself? At times it seems easier to express love, appreciation, and gratitude to others than to ourselves.

Here are a few ideas that will help you step up and nurture yourself:

1. Be optimistic about yourself, your abilities, and talents. Recognize that you make daily contributions.

2. Goals are good and help keep us focused. If a goal you set is not reached for whatever reason, do not allow this to diminish your value and self-esteem. Re-evaluate the goal, and make certain that it is reasonable and attainable.

3. Refusing requests is not wrong and should not cause you to feel guilty. You have the right to say *no*. You deny your own importance when you say yes and you really mean *no*.

4. Manage stressors in your life.

   - Get enough sleep.

   - Be aware of your well-being.

   - Eat healthy foods and exercise.

   - Pace yourself and be realistic about what you can accomplish.

   - Don't procrastinate.

   - Avoid bringing work problems home with you.

   - Daily take time for yourself. Read a book, take a walk, call a friend, or practice some form of deep relaxation exercise.

   - Resolve interpersonal conflict. Deal with feelings of anger towards yourself and others. Work through your frustrations and seek support from family, friends, and a professional therapist if necessary.

5. Recognize that the "little things" can make the "biggest" impact on your life. Make an effort to begin each day with a positive outlook and attitude.

6. Take time to share a smile with others and engage in laughter.

Is a hectic lifestyle preventing you from feeling joy? Commit to making one change today. Create a comfort zone for yourself by following these self-nurturing steps.

The Cost of Conflict

Conflict is defined as a difference of wants, needs, or expectations. The world is filled with people who have differences of wants, needs, and expectations. These differences may create interpersonal conflict.

Interpersonal conflict occurs with family members, friends, and in the workplace as a result of differences in beliefs, personality traits, or work ethics. There are ethical considerations that make interpersonal conflict problematic such as conflicts that include jealousy, competition, gossiping, or intimidation of others. Family members may disagree over shared responsibilities, living space, and household rules. Co-workers may disagree over managerial styles, workplace expectations, shared resources, and problem-solving tactics. Interpersonal conflict can lead to lost productivity and profits.

Most people don't intend to create conflict with others. It is in our best interest to keep communication healthy and amicable. The problems occur when we fail to use healthy communication and our words and actions become aggressive and hostile. In our dealings with others, problems occur when we fail to use a cooperative approach. Most of us do not intend to create conflict in our relationships, and often we are not aware that our own behavior is contributing to interpersonal problems. Conflict happens when we are annoyed and frustrated, when we are having a bad day, and are focused on our own needs at the expense of others'.

When conflict arises, it is critical to identify ways to resolve disagreements. It is important to recognize that communication can be verbal or non-verbal. We must also look at what we've contributed to the disagreement. Examine the ways in which our communication could have been less defensive and more effective. Once we have identified our part in the conflict, such as blaming, it is important to work on eliminating that specific behavior from our communication style.

Interpersonal conflict often occurs when individuals engage in hostile, aggressive behaviors. Aggressive behavior is seeking to dominate others and meet personal needs at the expense of others. To reduce conflict with others, it is important to understand and practice assertive communication. This is to effectively express needs and wants, satisfying personal needs but not at the expense of others. The following ideas will help reduce frustration and improve healthy communication.

- ✔ Keep body language consistent with verbal assertiveness.

- ✔ Be aware of your facial expressions. Assertive words with angry facial expressions will communicate aggression, not assertiveness.

- ✔ Identify your position by stating your thoughts and feelings about a solution to the problem.

- ✔ Use empathetic expressions by acknowledging the other person's feelings and viewpoint.

- ✔ Be an active listener by paraphrasing the other person's feelings and viewpoint.

- ✔ Brainstorm together by exploring alternative solutions.

Engage in healthy verbal communication by planning time to talk with out distractions and interruptions. Begin the conversation with a point of agreement. This will help to establish positive feelings up front and eliminate negative boundaries that may result in aggressive communication.

The cost of conflict is high. It creates stress, minimizes productivity, and can ruin relationships. Most often we create conflict unintentionally because we fail to use cooperative approaches to dealing with others. The first step to preventing interpersonal conflict is to engage in assertive communication by using effective language that communicates a trustful tone of reduced defensiveness.

> *Every conflict we face in life is rich with positive and negative potential. It can be a source of inspiration, enlightenment, learning, transformation, and growth—or rage, fear, shame, entrapment, and resistance. The choice is not up to our opponents, but to us, and our willingness to face and work through them.*
> —Kenneth Cloke and Joan Goldsmith

Move to the Next Level

Is JOY available for everyone? Absolutely! Joy is available for everyone.

We arrange our lives to feel joy. The well-known TV Host Oprah Winfrey said, "You feel real joy in direct proportion to how you are living your truth."

In my book, *Switching Lanes*, I explain joy this way: Joy is the sustained inner peace you feel when you find balance while moving your life in a positive direction.

Are you moving your life to the next level?

🧩 Happiness!

True or False:

- ✔ Research shows that most people are relatively unhappy.

- ✔ Wealthy people are more likely to be happier than those who are not.

- ✔ People who have children are happier than people without children.

- ✔ Healthier people are happier.

All of the above statements are **FALSE.** They are all reasonable and widely believed, but they are not supported by research to be true. Writers, social scientists, and the general public seem to believe that people around the world are dissatisfied and unhappy, yet scientific studies show the vast majority of people—even those who are poor or disabled—see themselves as fairly happy.

🧩 Color Your Life Happy

Do you find it difficult to feel happy? Are there days that, from the minute the alarm rings in the morning until you fall in to bed at night, feelings of happiness are non-existent? Why, you may ask? To answer this question, let's take a close look at what predicts happiness, what does not, and if genetics matter. You may be surprised.

Factors that do not predict happiness are:

Money: Recent research suggests that the correlation between actual wealth and people's perceptions of whether they have enough money to meet their needs is surprisingly modest. With persuasive advertising and escalating material wants, people feel that they cannot afford what they need and want; therefore, they feel dissatisfied with their income.

People are so focused on financial success that they don't derive much satisfaction from family life.

Higher income is associated with working longer hours, leaving less time for leisure pursuits.

Age: Age and happiness are consistently found to be unrelated. There may be a shift in focus as people become older—work becomes less important, and health becomes more important—but people's average level of happiness remains relatively constant over a lifetime.

Parenthood: Children can be a great source of joy and fulfillment, but they can also be a tremendous source of stress. Compared to childless couples, parents experience more marital problems. However, the positive and negative aspects of parenthood balance each other out, people who have children are neither more nor less happy than people without children.

Intelligence and Attractiveness: Intellect and physical attractiveness are highly valued by our society. Research has found no direct correlation between these characteristics and happiness.

Factors that do predict happiness are:

Love and Marriage: Romantic relationships can be stressful yet people identify being in love as a critical ingredient for happiness. Among both men and women, married people are happier than those who are single or divorced.

Work: Work is a source of happiness. Less critical than love and marriage, job satisfaction has a tremendous association with happiness. Studies also show that unemployment has a strong negative effect on happiness and well-being.

Do genetics influence happiness? The best predictor of a person's future happiness is their past happiness. Happiness does not depend on external factors as much as internal factors. Some people are destined for happiness and others are not. Genetic dispositions account for a substantial variance in happiness.

There are links between personality and well-being. People who are outgoing, upbeat, and sociable tend to be happier. Other personality traits that correlate to happiness include conscientiousness, agreeableness, self-esteem, and optimism.

Is happiness a state of mind? Research leads us to believe that genetics influence happiness.

The Secret to Happiness

Harvard professor and social psychologist, Dr. Daniel Gilbert, explains that when it comes to feeling happiness in our lives, at times we have the wrong map and our brain misjudges what makes us happy. We also make incorrect assumptions about what will make us happy, because we aim for the wrong things in terms of having happiness in our lives.

What's the secret to happiness? Past generations have felt that happiness is achieved when one gets what one wants. Generations of today have proven that to be incorrect. Large groups of people today have everything they want, and they are still not happy. Happiness is more than getting what you want.

Why do we aim for the wrong things? The answer lies in our inability to predict what we want in the future. Our mental life simulator has flaws when it comes to knowing what will make us happy five, ten, twenty years down the road. People cannot predict how their lives will be in future situations.

What are we doing wrong when it comes to being happy? When it comes to happiness, details matter. Too often our mental life simulator leaves out the details. Think about going to the dentist. What do you remember about the dental visit—the smell of the room, the sound of the drill, the pain from the shot? These are the negative aspects of the dentist. What about the positive details you experienced during your dental visit. For example, getting a close parking space, the friendly receptionist, and an inspirational article you read in the waiting room.

When it comes to being happy, all the details matter—the negative and the positive details. It is also important to recognize that we cannot predict our future happiness. We are convinced that our future happiness will be like our present experiences.

When it comes to happiness, we need to account for change in our lives. What we see as happiness at eighteen years old will not bring us happiness at twenty-eight years old. At age eighteen you may not see your life changing much by age twenty-eight. When you are twenty-eight years old, you will see that your life has changed a great deal in the past ten years. Predicted change and actual change are often not aligned. When we get to the present, we will no longer be living in the past. Happiness is strongly influenced by details and change.

Often we predict that an experience will be horrible, but the outcome actually brings us happiness. Sir Thomas Brown's theory—The Power of Rationalization—is the answer. We have the ability to rationalize. There is more than one way to look at a given situation. For example, you lose your job. At first this appears to be horrible. However, you may begin to rationalize that losing your job will bring the opportunity to do something else. You didn't like your job anyway.

People are resilient and do eventually recover from a traumatic situation like losing a job. When it comes to happiness, we are more resilient than we realized when faced with trauma in our lives.

What causes happiness? Mom would tell us that marriage, money and children bring happiness. Research tells a different story. Marriage causes happiness if the marriage is a good one. Money brings happiness but you do not need a lot of it. Children can be a source of joy and fulfillment, but raising children can also bring a tremendous amount of stress and hassles. Statistically, nonparents are happier than parents and parents are least happy when their children are younger. Even though the data shows that they don't bring happiness, we believe that children bring happiness.

To summarize, Dr. Gilbert states that brains and moms are fallible. Don't trust them—check out the facts for yourself. For me, happiness is based on personal perceptions of my life and how I feel about myself. Family, hard work, a spiritual connection and social belonging make my life happy and fulfilled.

Recharge!

Do you measure happiness by things rather than by moments? Take a few minutes and empower yourself through positive acts that will enhance your happiness.

- ✔ Work on a project that is meaningful to you.

- ✔ Give a compliment. Take time to cheer on a family member, colleague, or friend.

- ✔ Post an inspirational thought or quote on your bathroom mirror.

- ✔ Email a friend.

- ✔ Listen to uplifting music.

- ✔ Get moving. Talk a walk, attend a fitness class, or play an outdoor game with your kids.

- ✔ Help someone in need.

- ✔ Be grateful. Begin by listing the things you are grateful for. In a gratitude journal, express daily thanks.

- ✔ Read a chapter in an inspirational book that uplifts you. View the *Suggested Reading List* at the back of this book.

- ✔ Stop and enjoy the sunrise or sunset.

✔ Allow someone to move ahead of you while waiting in line at the bank or grocery store.

✔ Share a smile. A simple smile can brighten someone's day.

✔ Send a card to a family member expressing your love and appreciation.

✔ Spend time alone.

✔ De-clutter your living space. Give away something that you no longer need or want.

✔ Donate your time. Give service to your church or community.

✔ Take time to go through family pictures and appreciate the memories from past vacations and events.

✔ Watch an old movie.

Recharge and feel happy. Begin by arranging time in your schedule to enjoy outings with family and friends. Take time to uplift yourself, de-clutter your mind or living space, share a smile, your time, or send a card to brighten someone's day. Recognize the benefits of sharing simple acts of kindness.

Happy Days, Happy Nights

Stop cheating yourself of happy days and nights. Eating a poor diet, and lack of exercise and solid sleep may prevent you from being your best, looking healthy, and feeling optimistic.

Are you familiar with the phrase, "You are what you eat"? A balanced diet is an important step to staying healthy and reducing stress. You will feel healthier and happier when you maintain a balanced diet that contains a variety of nutrients. Making smart choices about what you eat will help ensure a healthier lifestyle.

Happy days and reduced stress come from eating a healthy, balanced diet. Improve your daily nutrition and overall health by following these tips:

✔ **The balancing act.** Find your balance between exercise and food. Stay within your daily calorie needs and exercise at least thirty minutes each day.

✔ **Go lean with protein.** Avoid foods that are high in saturated and trans fats and cholesterol. These foods raise blood cholesterol levels and increase the risk of heart disease and stroke.

✔ **Focus on fruits.** Eat two cups every day of fruits and limit your intake of fruit juices, which lack fiber and are high in sugar.

✔ **Mix it up and vary your veggies.** Enjoy a variety of vegetables, and don't forget dark green veggies like broccoli and spinach.

✔ **Limit sugar.** Choose foods and beverages low in added sugar. Added sugars pile on calories with few, if any, nutrients.

Happy nights come from sleeping well. A good night's rest can sharpen your focus, curb day-time food cravings, help you lose weight, aid your immune system, and help to increase optimism. Sleep tight and enjoy the benefits of a good night's sleep by following these tips:

✔ **Stop stimulants.** Limit your intake of coffee, tea, and cola for at least four to six hours before bedtime.

✔ **Say no to naps.** If you have trouble sleeping at night avoid napping during the day.

✔ **Turn off the noise.** Create a sleep environment that is pleasant and relaxing. Turn off the noise and light from phones, tablets, computers and the television.

✔ **Check your mattress.** Make sure your mattress is comfortable. Associate your bed with sleep and avoid doing work while you are in bed. This can make it difficult to unwind.

✔ **Dial-down the drama.** Avoid emotionally upsetting activities and stimulating or unpleasant conversations before bedtime.

Happy days and nights are the result of wise choices. Choose to balance your diet, increase your daily activity, and improve your sleep routine. By following these tips you will live longer, be your best, and stay happy!

Five Reasons to Let Go and Move On!

There are times in your life when letting go of guilt, negative relationships, and irrational beliefs will make you stronger, healthier and happier. Knowing when to let go and move on can be challenging. Timing is everything. Here are five reasons to help you know when it's time to make change and move on!

1. **Your trust is being broken.**

   - Trust is earned and needs to be valued.
   - Trust is a two-way street. If someone in your life is not trustworthy, do not count on them to be your friend.
   - Walk away from individuals whose words and actions are inconsistent.

2. **Your worth is not valued—in personal *or* professional relationships.**

   - Know and recognize your personal worth.
   - Empower yourself from within, and be true to yourself.
   - Above all, respect yourself, and do not settle for anything less from your family, friends or co-workers.

3. **Your voice is not being heard.**

   - Speak up for yourself. Don't have regrets.
   - If not given a chance to speak your mind, stop talking and recognize that some individuals will choose not to listen.
   - Your opinion is valuable—have the confidence to express it.

4. **You're not living in the present moment.**

   - Stop ruminating about and living in the past.

   - Learn from past experiences, forgive yourself, and move forward.

   - Life is about taking risks, making changes, and following your instincts.

5. **You're sacrificing your happiness for others.**

   - Don't allow others to determine your happiness by making more withdrawals than deposits in your "happiness account."

   - Happiness is a choice. Choose to feel joy in your life.

   - It is not your responsibility to make others happy.

We can benefit from these inspired words from actress Jane Seymour. "You have to count on living every single day in a way you believe will make you feel good about your life—so that if it were over tomorrow, you'd be content with yourself."

Plant Good Seeds

Each day we have the choice to share kind words and uplift others. This poem by Og Mandino, author and "sales guru," has an insightful message:

> *"I will not waste even a precious second today*
> *in anger or hate or jealousy or selfishness.*
> *I know that the seeds I sow—I will harvest,*
> *because every action, good or bad,*
> *is always followed by an equal reaction.*
> *I will plant only good seeds this day."*

What type of seeds will you plant today?

Lemons or Lemonade

For many, a better future seems to be an illusion.

Are you full of optimism? Do you see the glass as half-full? Do you have the ability to make lemonade from lemons? In other words, do you live on the bright side of life?

Optimism is a mental attitude. As an optimist, one expects the best possible outcome from any given situation. Optimism provides feelings of hope. Researchers find that an optimistic lifestyle causes certain advantages. Staying positive can improve physical and mental health, increase productivity and decrease stress.

Throughout the world, people believe that the future will be better than the past. Children look to a positive future as they play the childhood game "when-I-grow-up-I-want-to-be." Research tells us that adults and teens are just as likely to see the glass as half full.

Being an optimist has its advantages.

Persistence: Optimists don't give up easily, and they are more likely to achieve their goals.

Better Health: Optimists have a tendency to view set-backs differently than pessimists. They also have less stress and healthier lifestyles.

Self-belief: Optimists believe in themselves, and they expect good things to happen. They are willing to take risks and create positive events in their lives as a result of this mindset.

Higher Achievement: Scientific evidence shows that optimism may be hardwired by evolution into the brain. Optimists often work harder and earn more. Economists at Duke University found that optimists even save more of their annual income.

While optimists expect the best possible outcome from any given situation, it is also important that they view the outcome realistically.

Optimism can positively affect your mental and physical health. Are you ready to turn lemons into lemonade and to live on the bright side of life?

Optimism 101

Try this simple technique to change your outlook on life.

Martin Seligman, PhD, the father of positive psychology, gives a quick lesson on a classic optimism-boosting exercise, which he calls the ABCDEs. The goal, Seligman says, is to get you to stop thinking pessimistically, rather than teach you to start thinking optimistically (which rarely works). "This fix isn't instantaneous," he says. "But we've done studies on it involving thousands of subjects, and we know it's effective." So next time you experience a setback, walk yourself through these five steps.

A　**Name the *Adversity* or problem.**

　　(For example, I didn't get a call-back after my job interview.)

B　**List your *Beliefs*.**

　　These are your initial reactions to the problem. (The interviewer saw right through me. I don't deserve that position. And he could probably tell that I don't believe in myself. I'm sure the other applicants are much smarter, younger, and more qualified than I am.)

C　**Identify the *Consequences* of your beliefs.**

　　(I'm going to quit my job search so I don't have to suffer through this feeling of failure again.)

D　**Formulate a *Disputation* of your beliefs.**

　　Pessimistic reactions are often overreactions, so start by correcting distorted thoughts. (I probably didn't feel confident, because that position wasn't the best fit. It's only a matter of time before I can find an opportunity that's right for me. And now that I've had practice, I will be better prepared to present my best self.)

E   **Describe how *Empowered* and *Energized* you feel now.**

(I'm more motivated to keep looking for a job that makes me happy. I won't let fear stand in my way.)

Happiness is a state of mind. Choose to feel and be happy by arranging your life to see the "positives" each day. Optimism is where it begins. Joy is available for everyone—even you.

A Game Changer

Celebrate optimism!

It's time to celebrate the positives in your life. Optimists are more likely to achieve their goals, have better health, greater prosperity, and more happiness than pessimists. There are many simple strategies you can use to empower yourself and those around you. Begin today by taking **The Optimism Challenge.**

The Optimism Challenge:

Select an item from the list below and incorporate it into your daily routine for one month.

- ✔ **Focus on the bright side of life.** Challenge yourself to express only positives about yourself and others. Avoid the negatives and begin to feel happier. You will also inspire others to think positive.

- ✔ **Express thanks.** Find things you are thankful for each day.

- ✔ **Share words of praise**. Give a family member, friend, or co-worker a compliment. Remember to include yourself!

- ✔ **Sprinkle your world with positives.** Choose your favorite quotes, and post them throughout your home and in the work place. Feel joy as you and others reflect upon these messages.

- ✔ **Be polite and appreciative.** Take the time to express appreciation to others by saying *thank you*.

- ✔ **Use technology to spread optimism.** Post positive messages on your website or Facebook page.

- ✔ **Share a smile.** The average person smiles fifty times a day. Smile more and increase your happiness.

Optimism is a game changer—it is powerful and contagious. Look on the bright side of life and empower yourself and others.

Power of Perception

Perception is the cognitive interpretation of events. Your perception of events relates to your inner self. What you choose to focus on and perceive is a personal choice. It is selective awareness. Each day you are presented with many things to perceive and interpret. The selection process then follows. Along with the process of perceiving and interpreting you have the opportunity to make choices. Making choices can create stress or optimism.

Stress is perceived differently. Some see it as humorous and manageable while others see it as threatening. Reducing stress also varies among individuals. The bottom line is you have more control over stress than you may think.

When dealing with stress, the first step is to realize that there are good and bad, positive and negative elements to any stressful situation. An example of a stressor for me is waiting. Whether it's at the airport, the bank, or the doctor's office, I hate to wait! Yet, waiting is a part of life. The sooner I figure that out, the better. Waiting can cause my blood pressure to rise, or I can change my viewpoint about waiting and lower my blood pressure. Waiting can be seen as a positive, not a negative; it all comes down to my perspective. I can view waiting as an opportunity to think, ponder, observe, and study other people and their behavior. I can use it to make lists, balance my checkbook, catch up on my reading, or surf the Internet on my tablet. You never catch me without a magazine or book in my purse. The point is when given a choice I would not opt to wait but often times it is out of my control. What I can control is how I choose to perceive the situation.

There are circumstances in your life that are stressful. You may not like your boss. You may not feel you have enough leisure time. You may not like the way you look because of a few extra pounds. You may not enjoy living alone. You can control and change some stressful situations in your life. Others you cannot control; but you always have a choice about your reaction to the stress. You have the freedom to choose what to think and what to focus on. I once read an article about a heroic example that illustrates this point:

> *Bob Wieland, at 44, who lost both his legs in Vietnam and propelled himself with his hands and no wheelchair, completed the Marine Corps Marathon about 10:15 p.m. Sunday, 79 hours 57 minutes after he started Thursday in Arlington.*

Reading about Bob Weiland was a wake-up call for me. It was difficult to feel frustrated about the stressors in my own life.

Too often, we don't control our thoughts, allowing them to steer us down a negative path. We are taught to be critical rather than supportive. Focusing on the negative rather than the positive is a learned behavior and can be changed.

Listed below are seven ways to convert negative stress patterns into positive ones:

Be an optimist. Have a proper perspective and be realistic about stress. See the glass half full and not half empty. Focus on the positives and not the negatives of stress. You have more control than you think.

Have an attitude of gratitude. When faced with stress, stop and be grateful for the good things in your life. Too often we overlook the positives around us.

Stop and smell the roses. Enjoy the simple things. Take the time to celebrate yourself and your life.

When I was in my late teens I was on a hike with a friend in Jackson Hole, Wyoming. The day was warm and the Teton Mountains were majestic and awe inspiring. After twenty minutes of hiking my friend turned to me and said, "You are talking too much. You need to be quiet and experience the beauty of the scenery." I will never forget his words. He was encouraging me to stop and smell the roses—to celebrate life.

Learn to laugh. Humor and laughter have healthy benefits. Laughter results in both physiological and psychological changes that are good for you. The effects of laughter increase heart rate and respiratory activity resulting in the relief of anxiety, stress, and tension. Look for the humorous aspects of stress and you will be better able to manage daily stressors. Remember, there is an element of humor in most situations; you just need to find it.

Stop multitasking. Trying to perform more than one task at a time can be inefficient and stressful. Concentrate on one thing at a time, and celebrate the completion of each.

Be objective. View each life situation realistically and avoid catastrophic thinking while analyzing life events. Be accurate and avoid using words like devastating, horrific, or terrible to describe situations. Restructure or reword the description of life situations with words like difficult or challenging. This will help you see the event more realistically.

Recognize that life is always unfinished. It is unrealistic to think that your to-do list can be finished without another task presenting itself. Be realistic about daily tasks, and do not overload your schedule. Manage tasks and reduce stress.

There are many aspects of your life that you can control, but it is essential to recognize that you can't control every situation or event. The good news is that you can take control of yourself, your perceptions, and choices. Stress management requires confidence in yourself and your decisions to control your life. Recognize that with control comes responsibility. Take greater control of your life by being responsible for your behavior and accountable for your successes and failures.

Change your approach to stress, and be optimistic! The process of controlling your daily stress will increase your self-esteem and personal belief that leads to a successful lifestyle.

> *To get through the hardest journey we need take only one step at a time, but we must keep on stepping.*
> *-Chinese Proverb*

Go For It

Change the world one word at a time

Words express happiness, optimism, anger, frustration, disappointment, and much more. We use words every day to express our feelings, give direction, teach life skills, and build esteem in ourselves and others. Words are a pivotal part of our world. They begin as a thought and become powerful when spoken.

We are all profoundly affected by the way we use, hear, and interpret words. Family, friends, and colleagues are also impacted by our words and the way we choose to express ourselves. The power of words can contribute to or detract from our overall health. Words either hurt or heal.

We empower and demean through language.

Biased language includes expressions that degrade or exclude people because of age, sex, race, religion, social class, or physical or mental disabilities. When used, biased language risks alienating specific groups or people. Biased language also insults the person or group to which it is applied.

Gender-biased language favors a specific gender over another. Examples of gender-biased words are: manmade, mailman, or mankind. Change gender-biased language by using the following words:

> manmade = synthetic
> mailman = mail carrier
> mankind = humanity

Stereotyped language is any language that assumes a stereotype about a person or group of people.

Recognize that words cannot be retrieved. Once spoken or written, if inappropriate, damage control can begin through an apology or retraction. To avoid the mishap of using inappropriate words, here are a few suggestions:

- ✔ Alter negative speech patterns by not using words like stupid, ugly, or dumb.

- ✔ Avoid using biased language in any form.

- ✔ Speak positive words and share uplifting expressions.

- ✔ Give compliments. The process of complimenting others may seem awkward but will become more natural with practice. Giving a compliment takes nothing away from the giver and can be a life altering experience for the receiver.

- ✔ Explore ways to use effective communication to build esteem.

I once read that a word is like a living organism, capable of growing, changing, spreading, and influencing the world in many ways, directly and indirectly through others. Choose words wisely and recognize that we have the option to change the world for the better, one word at a time. Are you up for the challenge?

Power in Being Alone

We live in a world of commotion. There are countless numbers of distractions around us each day. Many people find it challenging to escape from the commotion in our world. Is solitude a luxury of the past? Do you welcome opportunities to be alone?

> *In an article by Susan Cain and in her recently released book,* Quiet: The Power of Introverts in a World That Can't Stop Talking, *she writes that research strongly suggests that people are more creative when they enjoy privacy and freedom from interruption. And the most spectacularly creative people in many fields are often introverted, according to studies by psychologists Mihaly Csikszentmihalyi and Gregory Feist. They're extroverted enough to exchange and advance ideas, but they see themselves as independent and individualistic. They're not joiners by nature.*

The ability to be alone reflects independence and self-sufficiency. Take time to be alone. You may find it works for you.

Evaluate Yourself

Are you an introvert or an extrovert?

Psychologist Carl Jung wrote in his book, *Psychological Types*, that introverts are drawn to the inner world of thought and feeling. Extroverts are drawn to the external life of people and activities. Introverts focus on the meaning they make of the events swirling around them and extroverts plunge into the events themselves.

Introverts are shy, reflective, thinkers. They are the ones who prefer listening to talking, reading to partying; who think before they speak and recharge their batteries by being alone. Introverts often work more slowly and deliberately, focusing on one task at a time.

Extroverts are assertive and social. They think out loud, enjoy meeting new people, and tend to tackle assignments quickly. At times, extroverts make fast (sometimes impulsive) decisions. Extroverts are comfortable with multitasking and recharge their batteries through socializing.

What are you?

Answering a few simple questions may help you recognize if you are an introvert or an extrovert.

✔ Do you prefer one-on-one conversations or group activities?

✔ Do you prefer expressing yourself in writing or verbally?

✔ Are you the life of the party, or do you sit back and take everything in?

✔ Do you prefer listening or talking?

✔ Do you prefer working on your own or with a group?

✔ Do you prefer focusing on one task, or do you prefer multitasking?

✔ Do you have a quiet kind of energy or high energy?

Today's psychologists describe **introverts** as being drawn to less outside stimulation with a quiet kind of energy. They prefer solitude, listening to talking, focusing on one task at a time, and they're not overly worried about wealth, fame or status. **Extroverts** tend to be assertive, high energy and the life of a party. They prefer talking to listening, are comfortable with conflict and multitasking and are drawn to social stimulation.

Behind Our Behavior

Today's psychologists agree that introverts and extroverts differ in the level of outside stimulation they need to function well.

Extrovert and introvert behavior is in our DNA.

We see more extroverts in America and Europe than in the Asian and African cultures. Researchers believe that populations that descend largely from those who migrated are more extroverted than those who did not.

EXAMPLES:

Introvert or Extrovert?

- ✔ **A PTA meeting**—members are discussing when to hold the Spring Carnival. A member speaks with enthusiasm and energy, "We must have it on the first Saturday of May. That is tradition. I see no other options."

- ✔ **Following a business conference**—attendees are discussing where they will go for dinner. One gentleman says in a quiet, reserved voice, "I am tired and need some down-time. I am going to return to my room, order room service, and unwind with a good book."

- ✔ **A husband and wife are discussing the family finances.** The wife says in an assertive voice, "I feel that our family needs a summer vacation. Time together as a family is important. We will cut back on other expenses to find the funds to take a vacation."

- ✔ **A group of teens are chatting about plans for Saturday night.** One teen quietly listens to several suggestions and then speaks up saying, "We always go to a movie; let's try something different like bowling."

What do you communicate to others about yourself?

Extroverts speak with conviction and are perceived as smarter than the introvert. This perception is not accurate. Often introverts have the best ideas because they have quietly gathered information and insight.

Too often the best presenters of the idea do not have the best idea, but because they voice their opinion they are seen as having the best idea.

However, there is no link between more talking and greater insight.

The world needs the introvert and the extrovert. The introvert brings an insightful, modest, reserved approach while the extrovert is outgoing, enthusiastic and has conviction. Both styles bring success!

Observe the Road Signs

Are you moving your life in a positive direction?

Placing puzzle pieces and observing road signs are similar: the process of doing both requires your attention. As you motor along the highway of life, there are road signs that give you insights, guidance, and direction. Other signs offer messages of warning. Are you coasting through life unaware of these signs or stuck in neutral along the roadside, unable to move forward?

Here are some dos and don'ts that may help. Shift your life into drive and begin to move forward. Get started by paying attention to all the "signs" in your life.

Balance first. Unbalanced tires on a car make for a rough ride. An imbalanced life does too. Find balance for yourself. Take time to relax, play, and serve. Life is not all about work. Give back to yourself, to others, and find joy through service.

Think negatively—be negative. It's all how you look at life. Reverse your thinking and change your perspective. We are what we think, so think positively.

Communicate clearly. The delivery of your message is the key. Speak up, get to the point, and say what you mean. Communication is more effective when done in a distraction-free environment and when all participants are engaged in listening. Too much time is wasted on miscommunication.

Micro-managing is a waste of time. Time is a precious commodity and, something most of us do not have enough of. Don't spend your time micro-managing yourself and others. You don't have to do it all. Feel confident that others can manage their share of the work load without your help. Micro-managing depletes others of their confidence and promotes inefficiency. Focus on effectively managing your share of the responsibilities, and don't second guess your ability to succeed.

Be true to yourself. Do not compromise your integrity or conform to other's ideas to be accepted. Walk away from individuals who ask you to be untrue to yourself.

Manage your to-do list. Writing a to-do list is an effective time management tool if you manage the list and the list does not manage you. Be realistic about your list and avoid overloading it with too many items. This will cause you to feel overwhelmed. Prioritize your list by arranging items from most important to least important. At the end of the day, if you haven't completed all the items on your list, move the most important tasks to tomorrow's list. An incomplete to-do list isn't a failure. View it as a jump start on tomorrow's tasks.

Material possessions are over-rated. We live in a society that measures our worth by the amount of stuff we own—a big house, a fast car, jewelry, club memberships. The list goes on and on. Too much energy is spent on collecting, spending, and managing worldly possessions. No wonder we are exhausted. Simplify your life and measure your worth by the good you do, not by the stuff you collect.

Keep your promises. Be realistic, and don't make promises that you cannot keep. It is important to be viewed by others as honest and trustworthy. Relationships, personally and professionally, are built on trust. You are only as good as your word.

Media driven images are an illusion. Try to avoid the urge to compare yourself to the cover of the latest fashion or fitness magazine. The photos featured on magazine covers and billboards are an illusion. They have been Photo-shopped, cropped, and manipulated to look "perfect." Perfection is not reality and should not be an expectation. It is what's inside you that really matters. Learn to gain confidence from within by recognizing your contributions and talents.

Move to the driver's seat of your life. Staying in the passenger's seat is risky. You may lose control of the direction your life will move. Observe all signs along the way and take the route that will lead you to a positive destination.

*With ordinary talent and extraordinary
perseverance, all things are attainable.
—Thomas Foxwell Buxton*

Celebrate optimism, live life to the fullest and THRIVE!

Take time to stop and smell the roses

Happiness is a state of mind

Recognize that you have more control than you think

Initiate opportunities to share your time through service

Validate yourself and others through compliments

Embrace change

Achieve Success

**Success can make you go one of two ways.
It can make you a prima donna, or it can
smooth the edges, take away the insecurities,
and let the nice things come out.**

-Barbara Walters

PUZZLE PIECES IN THIS SECTION:

The 'I' Concept

What are you communicating to others about yourself?

Begin by answering these four important questions:

1. How do I see myself?

    Personal perception is the key. How you perceive yourself and your contributions creates a foundation of confidence or self-doubt.

2. Am I one-dimensional?

    Adjust your perspective. If your perspective about your contributions and talents is imbalanced and negative then take the time to make adjustments. Recognizing your accomplishments will help you reclaim your confidence, so focus on the positives.

3. Do I define myself or am I defined by others?

    Embrace opportunities to re-define. Life is a process, and what you resist will persist. Do not allow others' opinions to define you and determine your success. Confidence comes by acknowledging insecurities, seeing beyond personal fears and embracing opportunities to stretch outside of your comfort zone.

4. Is my self-definition balanced?

    Take action and thrive. A quick fix to low self-esteem is to get into action. Fear will immobilize you if you allow it to. Choose to balance your life and your self-definition by moving forward and believing in yourself.

The "I" Concept is an introspective inventory of you. First, define your purpose, roles, and values. Next, take a closer look at your talents, strengths, flaws, and weaknesses. Finally, avoid focusing only on your vulnerabilities. Do not be blind to your assets. Allow this personal inventory to inspire you to live a confident, successful life. Buy a small journal and write it all down. Read it often—even daily. Share it with those you respect and are close to. Record your successes, and celebrate them by treating yourself to a small gift or have lunch with friends.

🧩 Smart Move

A personal logo, do you have one?

What is your personal logo, and what is it saying about you? Personal branding is essential in today's world. You build your brand daily.

Branding is one of the most important aspects of any business. The foundation of their brand is their logo. A company's logo is their promise to their customers. Their logo communicates their brand to the world. BMW's logo communicates to the world that they are the "ultimate driving machine."

Build a successful personal logo by following these steps.

- ✔ Be consistent in your message about yourself.

- ✔ Start from the inside out.

- ✔ Drive your own definition, and be true to yourself.

- ✔ Connect on an emotional level with yourself. Learn to empower from within.

- ✔ Be flexible. Recognize that your self-definition will change with adjustments in your life and lifestyle.

- ✔ Have clarity about yourself and your unique contributions.

Are you ready to create a personal logo that will empower you? A logo is a graphic representation of your brand. Eagles, lions, and wolves have been used as personal logos. So have hammers, musical instruments, and natural elements like trees and flowers. My good friend signs her name with a "smile" symbol to the left of her signature. This is her personal logo. If you are unable to draw the logo you may want to photocopy an image from a book or magazine or get it from the Web. To make it more real, you may want to tape it to the cover of your journal or place it on a white board in your home or office.

Impression Management

We live in an era of personal branding. Daily you brand yourself by what you wear, who you hang out with, your social media forums, and personal impressions. People desire to make positive impressions on others and to be liked. Warmth and competence are the two top impressions individuals seek.

Warmth reflects traits related to intent such as friendliness, morality, and trustworthiness. By contrast, competence is related to self-profitability traits like intelligence and skill. When we want to appear as warm we tend to agree, compliment, and encourage others. If we want to be seen as competent we emphasize our accomplishments, control the conversation, and exude confidence. Each goal is assisted with different behaviors. We care deeply about how warm and competent we appear to others.

A Princeton University research team found that those who appear warm often seem less competent, and those who convey competence generally come across as less warm. Their findings on downplaying positive impressions and the compensation between warmth and competence in impression management were published in the *Journal of Experimental Social Psychology*, September 11, 2012.

In their research, PhD. candidate, Deborah Son Holoien and psychology professor Susan T. Fiske found that there is an inherently negative relationship between being perceived as friendly and being perceived as competent. They stated that this causes people to stereotype societal groups—like different ethnic, religious, social, or gender groups—based on how warm they appear. Son Holoien and Fiske found that many groups tend to be characterized by ambivalent stereotypes related to mixed warmth and competence. For example, society views elders as friendly but incompetent and Asians as intelligent but cold.

Fiske explains that this trade-off is rooted in evolutionary theory. She is quoted as saying, "It makes sense because the first thing you need to know about another (is) what their intentions are. If their intentions are good, that means they're friendly and trustworthy and warm. The second thing you need to know is whether they can act on those intentions—whether they're competent and capable—because if they can't act on those intentions, they don't matter to you that much."

Fiske also found that these two characteristics have implications in business strategies and in the workplace. She stated that Johnson and Johnson, Campbell's, and Hershey are corporations seen by Americans as warm and competent. The energy and cigarette companies are seen as not only incompetent but also bad-intentioned. The luxury brands like Rolex and Porsche are perceived as cold and competent. Son Holoien and Fiske found that the two characteristics of warmth and competence determine 80 to 85 percent of impression formation. In daily interactions, these are the key things to be communicated. Fiske found through the research that how companies are viewed in light of these two characteristics affects what brands customers choose to purchase.

In today's society people are branding themselves by connecting locally and globally. Connecting through social and digital forums is gathering momentum as entrepreneurs use self-branding to benefit themselves and their businesses.

The power of the internet is growing and technology is becoming main stream, like switching on the light when you enter a dark room. Now is the time to take control of the branding process. Recognize that some individuals are naturally warm and others are confident and competent. Be true to yourself and package yourself correctly by recognizing the power of personal impressions.

What's Your *Signature Piece?*

While working in the fashion industry for fifteen years as a runway show choreographer, I noticed that most designers have a *signature piece*. Ralph Lauren's *signature piece* is the navy blazer.

What is your *signature piece*—your go-to talent, asset, or skill? Are you a good listener, an effective negotiator, productive under pressure or trustworthy and loyal?

To begin the process of identifying your *signature piece* it is important to evaluate your perceptions of yourself. Are they ambiguous? Do you send mixed messages to others about yourself? It begins with perception. Perceptions are your cognitive interpretation of incoming messages and the world around you. Perceptions are formed through observations, information in a visual form, and verbal and nonverbal messages.

The first step to identifying your *signature piece* requires taking a close look at the messages you send others about yourself. Are your messages clear or unclear? If they appear ambiguous, you must attempt to change the unclear messages that flow through your head by altering your mindset.

To alter your mindset you must be willing to change, avoid cognitive overload and limit distractions.

Change is a difficult process yet it is a constant in life. Learn to engage in positive change by seeing change as a challenge—not a threat.

When you view change as a CHALLENGE, you recognize and rely on your resiliency. Resiliency is the ability to identify and use your resources, strengths and assets to help you manage and master change.

When you view change as a THREAT, cognitive dysfunction takes place. You view change as black and white, which is restrictive and a one-sided perspective. You may engage in catastrophic thinking which results in negative thought patterns, and you will find yourself jumping to conclusions, becoming egocentric or using phrases like, *I can't change* or *I always fail at change.*

The second step to altering your mindset involves cognitive overload. We live in a world of choices and experience cognitive overload each day. To avoid cognitive overload you must manage your cognitive resources and choices. Too many choices will fuel anxiety, create stress, and limit productivity. Apply the technique of *thought stopping* to limit overload. Thought stopping is when you mentally shut off choices that are negative, inappropriate, or unproductive. Focusing on the right choices vs. good choices will help you identify those that will increase personal productivity.

Next you'll want to recognize and limit distractions. Distractions minimize progression. To limit distractions engage in the technique of *environmental planning.* Environmental planning occurs when you make adjustments to your life and environment by turning off your cellphone, identifying a specific time in your daily schedule to return emails, and organizing your work space. Don't fall victim to the technology trap! Distractions curtail productivity.

If identifying your signature piece is difficult for you, you are not alone. Most people find this process difficult. A signature piece can be a tangible item, a personality trait, or both. When my dad was alive, his signature piece was his wonderful sense of humor. He was also known for the T-shirts he wore to work with humorous sayings or pictures printed on the front of them. He was known for his collection of shirts and quick wit. My friend Jamie's signature piece is her loyalty to business associates, family and friends. This trait has helped her to build a very successful networking business. People trust Jamie because of her loyalty. Identify your signature piece and allow it to empower you. Don't hide behind low self-esteem, self-doubt, and a lack of self-efficacy, unfocused priorities, or negative thoughts.

To meet success with this process, look beyond your personal boundaries and shift your perspective about yourself, your strengths, and your talents. Focus on your attributes, and don't hide behind your vulnerabilities or be blind to your assets. Give yourself credit instead of discrediting yourself. Identify one key asset and build from there. Write it down and post it on your bathroom mirror or in your journal as a reminder of your *signature piece*.

As your life unfolds, you create a beautiful tapestry that is unique. It takes form, one stitch at a time, woven carefully and intricately into its own pattern. No two tapestries will reach completion at the same time, and each design will be uniquely different.

With any great work of art there will be varying stages in the design. There will be strokes of great brilliance and those that are less ostentatious. This is what gives each tapestry depth and beauty.
—Dehbe Collett

Express Yourself

If you have trouble saying no and feel like people walk all over you, then it is time to understand assertive communication.

Assertive communication is the ability to honestly express your feelings or opinions without anxiety or anger. It should not be confused with aggressive behavior.

Assertive behavior is clear and direct communication. Assertiveness is about being responsible for yourself, and making your life work for you, instead of being a victim of circumstances. It promotes feelings of confidence, midway between being a bully and feeling like a doormat.

You may find it difficult to use assertive communication. If so, you are not alone. Many people are uncomfortable with speaking assertively. The following tips will help:

> ✔ **Use assertive body language.** Face-to-face communication is important. Stand or sit straight, keep eye contact, and be serious but pleasant.

> ✔ **Act and speak assertively.** Avoid adding qualifiers to your opinions and feelings.

> ✔ **Take responsibility for yourself and your actions.** Use "I" statements. I feel… I am… I want….

> ✔ **Talk about the problem.** Don't blame or accuse others. Focus on the facts.

> ✔ **Allow time to cool down.** Defuse an unproductive outcome.

> ✔ **Be persistent with your request.** Avoid arguing or being manipulated.

Assertive behavior is dependent on a feeling of self-efficacy, knowing that if you act a certain way, something predictable will occur.

Be Inspired! Step Forward and Advocate

Self-Advocacy is to understand your strengths, needs and effectively communicate them to others. Well practiced advocacy skills will increase your chances of getting what you want.

You may ask: why advocate? It is important to understand the meaning behind advocacy and the benefits of advocating. Advocacy is the act of pleading or arguing in favor of something. It is a type of problem solving.

There are different types of advocacy:

> ✔ System advocacy is used to change the system and to promote a cause.

- ✔ Legal advocacy is what lawyers are paid to do. Advocate within the boundaries of the legal system.

- ✔ Legislative advocacy is used to change the laws.

- ✔ Self-advocacy is speaking up for yourself.

Self-advocacy refers to an individual's ability to effectively communicate or negotiate one's own interests, needs, and rights. Self-advocacy is recognizing your strengths and needs, knowing your legal rights and communicating them to others. Well practiced advocacy skills will increase your chances of getting what you want.

Self-advocacy skills help:

- ✔ avoid and solve problems with family members, associates, co-workers, neighbors,

- ✔ obtain reasonable and necessary accommodations in both public and private settings,

- ✔ identify, analyze and make informed decisions concerning personal choice,

- ✔ gain essential tools for defining and resolving problems, and

- ✔ empower you to gain more control over your life.

Steps to effectively advocate for yourself:

- ✔ Recognize that you have a voice. Take time to speak up.

- ✔ Value yourself, and see yourself as an equal. Your opinion counts so share it.

- ✔ Identify and define your request. Get to the heart of the problem.

- ✔ Distinguish the major issues from the incidental details.

- ✔ Educate yourself, and build expertise. Before advocating, do your homework.

- ✔ Set boundaries, and don't allow others to intimidate you.

✔ Find a mentor to help and give you support.

✔ Separate your passions from your emotions.

✔ Attitude is important. While advocating for yourself, or for others, be friendly but firm.

✔ A positive attitude about your advocacy efforts is critical to your success.

Learning to effectively advocate and speak up for yourself will increase your self-esteem and boost your confidence. You will recognize that your voice and opinion count. You will also have the ability to set personal boundaries and not allow others to intimidate you. Effective self-advocacy creates a feeling of empowerment and builds a life of sustained clarity and fulfillment.

Change It Up

Do you resist change?

Change is difficult, and it is hard work to modify behavior. We are creatures of habit, and change forces us out of our comfort zone. Fear and distractions also prevent us from making change.

Before you attempt to alter a behavior it is important that you answer the following questions:

✔ What behavior do I want to change?
✔ Why is change important to me?
✔ How will I benefit from this change?

After you select the behavior you want to change, you must be specific with your objective. This will help you to stay focused and to have clarity about the outcome. The following steps will help you implement change:

✔ **Have a realistic plan.** A realistic plan drives success. Make sure that your objective is achievable. For example, the goal to lose 20 lbs. in a week is not realistic or attainable.

✔ **Recognize barriers.** Ask yourself, what can I foresee that may lessen my ability to change my behavior and have success? *Time* is an example of a barrier. Your schedule may already be over committed. *A lack of energy* may be a potential barrier because of the long hours you spend at work. Removing barriers and redefining your goal may be necessary steps to making successful life change.

✔ **Establish reinforcements and punishments.** Recognize that punishments decrease behavior and reinforcement increases behavior. Reinforcements are rewards. They can be small and are more effective if given closer in time—daily or weekly. If your goal is to begin an exercise program, it is critical to adjust your daily schedule to include physical activity. When you stick with your plan, reward yourself. If you are unable to stay focused on your goal then enforce a punishment. A punishment helps prevent a negative outcome.

✔ **Set-backs will occur.** Don't give up. Social support may be needed to help you remain on task. Remember you can't rely on willpower alone. If you have set-backs, recognize that self-regulation is a key component to change. If you detour from your plan you may be distracted or fearful of the change. Review your plan and reshape it by making the necessary adjustments.

Change is a constant in life. Find strategies to help you make positive change. You control your choices and can make effective change in your life if your plan is realistic, and if you have a sincere desire to alter specific behaviors. Find the barriers that are preventing you from moving forward and achieving success.

I have created the **Resistance to Change Questionnaire** to help you identify personality traits that may be preventing you from adjusting to change.

Resistance to Change—Questionnaire

Rate yourself with a yes or no response. The following statements involve your perceptions about yourself, feelings and behaviors. A YES response denotes agreement about the behavior and a NO response denotes disagreement about the behavior.

1.	I am often talkative.	YES	NO
2.	I am original, and I come up with new ideas.	YES	NO
3.	In most situations I am not reserved.	YES	NO
4.	I often make plans and don't follow through with them.	YES	NO
5.	I am generally relaxed and handle stress well.	YES	NO
6.	I am curious about many things.	YES	NO
7.	I am flexible in most situations.	YES	NO
8.	I have an active imagination.	YES	NO
9.	I am inventive.	YES	NO
10.	I value artistic and aesthetic experiences.	YES	NO
11.	I am not shy.	YES	NO
12.	My choices often favor the group.	YES	NO
13.	I do not become nervous easily.	YES	NO
14.	I am politically liberal.	YES	NO
15.	I prefer to cooperate with others.	YES	NO
16.	I am helpful and unselfish with others.	YES	NO
17.	I generally bring a lot of energy to the group.	YES	NO
18.	I am open-minded.	YES	NO
19.	I see myself as a good listener.	YES	NO
20.	In most situations I am easy going.	YES	NO

Results: The higher your NO responses, the greater your resistance to change.

After completing the **Resistance to Change Questionnaire**, you may notice a pattern in your behavior that inhibits forward progression and adaptability to life changes. This exercise will help you recognize personality traits that may prevent you from successfully making change. It is important to recognize these behaviors can be altered, helping you to make effective change in your attitudes and lifestyle. Take time to change it up!

Recycle Yourself!

Convert Fear to Freedom

The fashion industry is masterful at recycling trends. If you loved a specific style 20 years ago, you may find it hanging on the store racks today. Recycling is a process, an evolution; it's taking the old and creating the new. There are very few originals in life. You can learn from the fashion industry and RECYCLE personal trends and your lifestyle by engaging in positive change.

Change is difficult and can be viewed as expected or unexpected in nature. **Expected change** is planning for and inviting change into your life, like attending graduate school, buying a new home or beginning an exercise program. **Unexpected change** is uninvited and not easily embraced. It is inconvenient change, like having a sick child on the day you have a million things to do or losing your job because of a sluggish economy.

Recognize that change is a constant in life. Some change you choose and some change comes at you like a tidal wave—it's not a choice. Losing your job is an unexpected change that causes feelings of fear and frustration. Choosing to relocate because of a job promotion is an expected change that may also create frustration and fear.

In order to embrace change it is important to answer the following question: Do I resist change and why? Like many people, you may fall victim to one or more of the following barriers that prevent you from making successful change:

- ✔ fear of the unknown

- ✔ viewing change as frustrating, overwhelming, or inconvenient

- ✔ the "buy in" isn't high enough, so making the change isn't worth your time or energy because the outcome is not important to you or a priority

- ✔ limited time or personal/financial resources necessary to make successful change

- ✔ lack of self-control and discipline

Engage in positive change by practicing the following:

Choose to act or react. When it comes to change you have two choices—to *act* or react to change. It is best to act and not react. Reaction is a knee-jerk response to change, and acting is a controlled choice.

Stretch yourself by altering your mindset about change. Temperament and personality can play a role in how effectively or ineffectively you deal with change. Researchers often refer to temperament as that which is inborn and biological based and personality as that which emerges from cultural influences and personal experiences. Temperament = nature and personality = nurture. Nature and nurture both contribute to an individual's resistance to change.

The good news is you can alter your mind set and perception of change, however; it's important to recognize that you can stretch your personality only to a certain point. Our inborn temperaments influence us regardless of the lives we lead. Susan Cain refers to this as "the rubber band theory" of personality in her book, *Quiet: The Power of Introverts in a World That Can't Stop Talking.* She claims that we are elastic and can stretch ourselves, but only so much. A sizable part of who we are is built into our genes, our DNA, yet we have freewill and can use it to shape our personalities. We want the freedom to map our own destiny through change, yet we have limitations due to our DNA and temperament.

Understanding how temperament and personality both influence resistance to change will help you when it comes to dealing with personal change and change that affects others—including your family, work colleagues, and members of your church or community. It is important to remember that successful change occurs when you make change for yourself and not for others. Resistance often occurs when change is forced upon you.

Convert fear to freedom: The key to converting fear to freedom is to view change as a challenge not a threat.

Individuals rely on their resiliency when they recognize change as a challenge. Resiliency is the ability to identify and use your personal resources, strengths and assets to help you master change.

When you view change as a threat, cognitive dysfunction takes place. You may view change as black and white. This is a restrictive, one-sided perspective of your options when faced with lifestyle change. Catastrophic thinking, exaggerating and jumping to negative conclusions are counterproductive. You may hear yourself saying, "I can't make successful change" or "I always fail at/resist/ dread change in my life."

Look beyond your personal boundaries: Take time to limit your anxiety by shifting your perspective. Avoid ambiguous messages about change and adjust your mindset by recognizing that negative ideas about change may or may not be true.

Successful change is possible. Distance yourself from negatives and recognize that criticism promotes low self-esteem. Stop dreaming about making positive change in your life and make a realistic action plan. Stop and recognize that "what ifs" create feelings of disappointment. Always give yourself credit instead of discrediting your abilities.

Take the challenge to recycle yourself and your lifestyle. It begins with taking the familiar, making a few changes and creating the new, improved you!

🧩 Good, Better, Best!

Make change and move your life from good to best. To begin this process it is important to take a look at the definition of these three words.

> **Good**—better than average
> **Better**—more desirable, more favorable
> **Best**—most excellent, surpassing all others

Whether it's an academic, professional, or personal rating, most would agree that an excellent rating is more desirable than a rating that is just average. The challenge in achieving the highest rating begins with two questions: Do I want to perform at the highest level? and Why is it important to me?

Here are some steps that will help you attain the best your life has to offer.

✔ **Move past regrets.** Learn from your mistakes, but don't allow these regrets to decrease your confidence and paralyze you from moving forward. I have a friend, Connie, who told me about her struggle with regrets of the past. She had been divorced when her children were young, and she was afraid she might have injured them emotionally as a result. She was also feeling guilty about the divorce, and the event had scarred her deeply. She felt that her dwelling on regrets was keeping her from moving on personally and professionally.

Connie told me she had found an unusual memorial park near her home. A place of peace and beauty, the park was created to ease the emotional pain of loss from cancer. It is non-denominational and open to anyone suffering from grief. She had heard about a small building that featured something called "The Bridge of Regrets." Outside was a small foot bridge over a little brook leading to a small raised firepit. Inside the softly lit building were wooden benches for meditation. A table in the corner held pens and pads of paper and a sign that read:

"Now is the time to release the regrets of the past, to break free from the debilitating pain of regret. Write down those thoughts that keep you from living a full life. Walk over the bridge, and burn your paper in the firepit. Watch your regrets vanish in the smoke. You have crossed the bridge into your new life of relief and liberation."

Not everyone has a memorial park like this nearby, but you, too, can symbolically free yourself from feeling regret using a similar "ceremony." Be sure to record the event in your journal and give yourself a great deal of credit for taking the initiative to break the habit of recalling regrets and negative thoughts about yourself and your actions in the past. Ask yourself this simple question, "If I were to turn back the clock, what would I change about myself and my life?" Once you have your answer to this question, go to work and make changes. Making change will prevent future regrets, which is the next point.

✔ **Avoid future regrets**. Spend less time on superficial things in life and focus on the best "stuff" life has to offer. Embrace meaningful experiences and people in your life.

✔ **Spend more time with the people you love.** Build deep connections with people who mean the most to you. Schedule "face time" with these individuals. Don't rely on the click of a text or the forwarding of an inspirational email to replace face-to-face conversations and outings. Don't be so overscheduled that you miss opportunities to connect with family and friends. Build relationships with those you love and care about. Link to others on a personal level; don't rely only on technology.

✔ **Unfinished business.** Do you feel like there are things in your life that are left unfinished? Maybe you feel that you've failed to live up to your potential. If this is the case, the good news is that it's not too late to complete unfinished business in your life and reach your potential.

First, recognize that life's journey is more than climbing a ladder to success. Success is found in the process of climbing, not about reaching the top. Success is not about completing the task or goal but about the process of learning and gaining personal growth. Take time to applaud your small successes in each day.

✔ **Be an active participant in your life.** Don't be a spectator. Determine the direction your life is moving. Don't dip your toe in the water and think you've gone for a swim. You need to jump into the water to begin swimming. Jump into your life, engage, and be committed to your life goals and daily experiences.

✔ **Connect to the moment.** Life is not to be appreciated in retrospect. Embrace each moment—positive or negative. We learn great lessons through adversity, and difficult times make the positive moments in life even brighter. It is essential to find value in the present moment and not to focus only on the finish line.

✔ **Let yourself be happy.** External circumstances don't determine happiness. Strong predictors of happiness include:

- feeling loved
- a sense of belonging
- hard work

Resolve to be joyful regardless of your circumstances. Regrets of tomorrow can be prevented by making the best choices today.

The **best** requires you to side-step better and jump over good. It is defined as most excellent, superior, and in order to accomplish excellence you must be disciplined and focused. In the end the sacrifices and adjustments you choose to make will be worth it. Good, better or best—it is your choice.

> *The road of life twists and turns, and no two directions are ever the same. Yet our lessons come from the journey, not the destination.*
> *-Dr. Don Williams, Jr.*

Emotion and Motivation

What is emotion?

Emotion is associated with mood, temperament, personality, disposition, and motivation. We all have many experiences that involve emotion, but it is a difficult concept to put into words. There are over 550 words in the English language that describe emotions, but we find it difficult to describe our own emotions.

The most profound experiences in life involve emotion. Emotions are part of our everyday experiences and are a highly personal experience.

Are we able to turn our emotions on and off like a switch?

No. If it were that simple then we could choose to be happy all the time. Emotions are feelings that happen to us rather than feelings we choose to make happen.

Research tells us that some degree of emotional control is possible, however; emotions tend to involve automatic reactions that are difficult to regulate.

What are "mixed emotions"?

Mixed emotions involve experiencing both pleasant and unpleasant feelings about the same event.

Example: You have just received a promotion at work. You feel **happiness** about the opportunity and **anxiety** regarding the challenging new responsibilities.

What is motivation?

Motivation is an internal condition that involves goal-directed behavior. It is the desire to do things. Research shows that you can influence your own levels of motivation.

The Three A's of Motivation are:

- ✔ **Achievement**—goal setting, reaching the goal builds self-esteem

- ✔ **Affiliation**—a sense of belonging, feelings of attachment build trust

- ✔ **Aggression**—persistent, bold, and energetic pursuit of furthering one's end

What motivates people to push themselves? A need for achievement, to be the best they can be.

Hard work is not the only determinant that drives achievement. Situational factors and incentives can also influence an individual's desire to achieve.

An example of this is when you work hard to earn an A in calculus class because you value good grades. There is also an incentive offered by your parents—the use of the family car for social activities if an A in calculus is earned.

Motivation and emotion are often intertwined. Emotion can cause motivation. An example of this is when the emotion of **anger** over your work environment may motivate you to look for a new job. Motivation can cause emotion. To illustrate this point, your motivation to win the community speech contest may lead you to feel **anxiety** over the competition. The outcome of the competition will cause you to feel either **elation** if you win or **disappointment** if you lose.

Motivation is an essential component to achieving success. Here are seven steps to help you take action and motivate yourself:

- ✔ Have clarity of your goal. Clarity is about *clearly* recognizing what you want and how to obtain it.

- ✔ Think positively. Surround yourself with positive thoughts and motivated people.

- ✔ Live healthy and avoid exhaustion. Get enough sleep, exercise and eat healthy food. This will help you have the necessary energy to take action.

- ✔ Own your personal choices, and avoid excuses.

- ✔ Recognize set-backs as an opportunity to learn—not to quit.

- ✔ Use action words like *I will or I must*. Do not use *I will try*. These three words give you permission to fail.

- ✔ Avoid procrastination. Achievement is met by taking action and meeting your goals. Empower yourself by choosing to succeed daily.

Motivation and emotion are closely related and may intertwine, but they are not the same thing. Both are multi-dimensional and not always predictable or manageable.

Recognize that you can influence your own levels of motivation and success. Think positive and be the best you can be. Continue to increase your self-esteem by taking steps to increase personal motivation.

Thinking Toolbox

Vision, attention, memory, and decision making are the toolbox of how we think in the real world. The process of thinking begins with how we perceive the world, and perception of the world is much more than just seeing the world.

Perception is the process of organizing and interpreting information around us. All day long we select objects and events for analysis. We take this information and give it meaning. Our perception of the world around us is influenced by our feelings and past experiences. Organizing and interpreting information is the way we gain knowledge. Expectations also influence our perceptions.

How do we perceive the world? In order to answer this question we must take a close look at our personal feelings, expectations, and past experiences. All three may influence and determine our interpretation of the information we are processing and thinking about. It is also important to be aware of personal bias. A bias is a prejudice in favor or against one thing, person, or group compared with another, usually in a way to be considered unfair.

Personal bias can also influence the processing of information, our behaviors and may cause an unwanted outcome. During a corporate training session I conducted on change and conflict, a female employee approached me following the morning session of the seminar. During our conversation she referred to her male colleagues as inflexible and self-centered. She felt that their rigid viewpoints and behavior were preventing positive momentum for the team. As our conversation continued I learned that she had recently been through a difficult divorce from a man she described as inflexible and self-centered. Her personal bias toward her ex-husband was affecting her feelings about all men, including the men she worked with. It is important to recognize that how we perceive the world becomes our reality.

Are we focused and attentive? We live in a fast paced world, full of information to perceive and process. Attention is the process of selecting objects and events in the world for conscious analysis. The key word here is conscious. It is important to note that in order to remember and recall information we must pay attention. All day long we select certain information to focus on, remember, and attend to. The challenge is staying focused long enough to process the incoming information. Distractions make it difficult to focus and pay attention. The process of focusing and attending to incoming messages is simple—we must **attend** to the information to remember the information. In other words, focus, listen, and eliminate distractions while attending to incoming messages from family, friends, and work associates. The process sounds simple, but listening and attending to information can be a constant challenge in a world full of sound and visual overload.

Why is it difficult to recall information? The answer to this question is simple—retrieval cues—the process of accessing memories. We find it difficult to recall information from our memory because we lack the appropriate content to retrieve that information from our memory.

In spite of memory's numerous benefits, it can also let us down. "Memory, for all that it does for us every day…for all the feats that can sometimes amaze us, can also be a troublemaker," said Daniel Schacter, PhD, longtime memory researcher and author of *The Seven Sins of Memory: How the Mind Forgets and Remembers.*

Memory relies on the ability to effectively retrieve information that is accessible and available. It begins with focusing on incoming information and properly storing it. Inability to retrieve memories is caused by forgetting, poor processing of the information, distractions, or distorted and unwanted memories.

Do we make optimal decisions? The answer to this final question is no, not always because many of our decisions are irrational. Most people attempt to be rational and systematic in the decision making process; however, the problem is they apply simple strategies in decision making and focus only on a few available options. This approach may result in decisions that are less than optimal.

It is critical to understand how we think in the real world. The ability to focus, recall information, and make optimal decisions will increase self-esteem and lead to feelings of competence. Rely on the thinking toolbox to help you block out distractions, pay attention to incoming messages, and manage cognitive overload while living in a fast-paced world.

Think Outside the Box

Think outside the box is a common phrase and one we are all familiar with. This phrase refers to "creative thinking" to solve difficult problems, and it encourages you to move outside of your comfort zone. Moving outside of your comfort zone can be frightening because leaving the "familiar" to step into the "unknown" is risky and difficult.

Here are some ideas to help you think outside the box:

- ✔ **Be open-minded.** Having an open mind is essential to succeed in life—personally and professionally. Considering new ideas is vital to personal growth and successful living. It is important to look at new information and facts without bias.

- ✔ **Take time to listen.** To embrace new ideas, you must be willing to listen and consider others' ideas. Recognize that there is more than one way to accomplish a goal. Be flexible and willing to evaluate new perspectives.

- ✔ **Ask questions.** Before deciding that a new idea isn't the answer, ask questions for clarification. Do additional research if necessary, and be willing to step outside your personal boundaries of confined thinking.

- ✔ **Remove barriers.** Don't think that you have to be right all the time. Avoid skepticism or disbelief in regard to a new approach or idea. Remember, there are several different ways to get things done. Don't allow unfamiliar ideas to hold you back from thinking creatively and solving difficult problems.

- ✔ **If it doesn't work, fix it.** This will require action steps. You may need to take on new tasks and responsibilities and be willing to approach the problem from a different angle. Developing skills that help you think and act differently will require effort. To see things in a new way, you must be willing to alter your thinking and step outside your boundaries.

My neighbor, Laurel, experienced this first hand when she was forced to go through job transition because her company downsized, and she lost her job. Laurel is a soft spoken introvert who finds it difficult to network and multi-task. In order to find a job, she found herself developing new skills, stepping outside of her "comfort zone," and learning to advocate for herself. Laurel was successful because of her willingness to make change, expand her boundaries, and approach the problem from a different angle.

Thinking outside the box will require you to make changes by leaving the familiar path. By establishing new boundaries, you will unlock new ways of thinking and begin to feel empowered. Being open-minded will help you to be flexible, learn new things, and strengthen your skills. Recognize that expanding your comfort zone will help you to look beyond your established boundaries, accept new challenges, and ultimately be more successful.

Outside the Lines

Master effective decision making

When it comes to making decisions, do you feel nervous, anxious or overwhelmed? What barriers are preventing you from making effective decisions in your life—personal or professional?

Often times, the process of making a decision can be paralyzing. Indecision plagues even the greatest leaders and entrepreneurs. Here are five steps that will help you become an effective decision maker:

✔ **Decide to decide.**

Effective decision-making skills will increase personal productivity. Spending time worrying about making the wrong decision is counterproductive and a waste of time. Approach each decision that needs to be made with a positive attitude. Decide to decide; this is the first step towards preventing indecision and avoidance in your life.

✔ Trust your instincts.

Listen to your inner voice and trust your instincts. There lies a wealth of knowledge in past experiences. Don't mistrust all emotion-driven decisions.

✔ Less is better.

When it comes to making decisions, avoid the desire to gather outside perspectives. Input from a few people is wise, but only to a certain degree. Too much information only complicates the decision-making process. It is helpful to look at different options and to gather various perspectives; however, when it comes to effective decisions, there are times when less input is better.

✔ Permission to choose again.

The right choice or the good choice: which is the best choice? Life offers us many good choices. Look at all your options and select the choice that is right for you at that time and place in your life. This decision will move you forward, keep you focused, and help you be successful.

It is important to remember that if this choice proves to be wrong, you have permission to choose again. Do not look at an incorrect choice as a failure. It is simply an opportunity to learn, readjust, and make the right choice.

✔ Focus blurred boundaries.

Successful decisions begin with focused boundaries. Prioritize your fears. Don't allow your fear of past poor choices inhibit your ability to make positive decisions now. Poor choices are in the past, so keep them there. Aim high, and be true to yourself. Don't allow others' negative opinions influence you to take a lower path.

Effective decision-making skills will empower you and increase your personal productivity. Avoidance is a barrier that prevents forward progression. Indecision is all about avoiding the opportunity to make a choice to select a direction and take action. Look outside the lines for answers and remember, in the end the choice is yours.

Be More!

Are you overwhelmed by countless choices?

Decisions, decisions, decisions—life is full of decisions. Each day you make many decisions. Earlier today you decided when to wake up, what to eat for breakfast, and what clothing to wear to work. These decisions were probably easy, requiring little effort. Occasionally, you will need to make big decisions that will require time and may be difficult. Big decisions like buying a home, car, or changing jobs have many different facets that need to be evaluated and weighed.

Decision making involves making a choice after evaluating all the available alternatives and options. Most people try to be rational and systematic in this process. They apply simple strategies in decision making and focus on only a few available options. This approach may result in decisions that are less than optimal. Research tells us that people do not always make rational decisions.

Many decisions involve choices about preferences. Theorists argue that people in modern societies are bombarded by an overabundance of choices about preference. Psychologist, Barry Schwartz, showed that a simple trip to the grocery store can require a consumer to choose between 285 varieties of cookies, 61 suntan lotions, 150 lipsticks, and 175 salad dressings. Although increased choice is most apparent in the realm of consumer goods, Schwartz argues that it also extends into more significant areas of life.

In today's world individuals have many opportunities about how they will live, where they will work, and how they will spend their money. It is clear that we may feel overwhelmed with countless choices. Here are a few strategies to help you make optimal decisions:

Write it down. Making a list and working on a physical plane of paper and pencil make it easier for you to sort out issues. Too many ideas rolling around in your head can confuse you, allow you to forget important points, and hinder your decision-making progress.

Evaluate the positives. List and evaluate all the alternatives. Indicate the positive attributes of each alternative that will influence your decision. Rate the alternatives based on the positive attributes.

Eliminate by negatives. Make your choice based on gradually eliminating less-attractive alternatives. When an alternative fails to satisfy some criterion for an attribute, eliminate it from the list.

Don't be impulsive. Take the time to evaluate and explore all your options. Do your homework and collect enough data to make a rational choice. Take it one step at a time, and select alternatives that will lead you to the optimal decision. Do not fall victim to taking chances that result in risky decisions.

Avoid conditions of uncertainty. Risky decisions are often the result of making choices under conditions of uncertainty. Rely on background knowledge and past experiences to help you make rational choices.

People rely on different modes of thinking when it comes to making rational decisions and the approach may vary with each situation, so the key to avoiding choice overload is to select strategies that work for you.

STOP and Alter Your Mindset

Successful living isn't about adding skills, money or "things" to your life. It's about changing behaviors and habits that promote a negative outcome.

Six steps to successful living:

✔ **Stop waiting!**

How do you spend your time? Are you waiting to be happy, healthy or successful?

It is important to recognize that how you spend your time defines you. If you are spending too much time waiting, then it's time for CHANGE! Make change in your life by setting a goal and creating a realistic plan to achieve that goal so you can move forward. Stop waiting for things to happen, and begin to make things happen.

✔ **Stop blaming others!**

Do you blame others for your mistakes or failures?

Nobody wins at the "blame game." Take responsibility for your thoughts, choices, and actions. It may seem easier to point the finger at someone else instead of owning it yourself. In the long run you will learn more from your mistakes than passing them off as someone else's fault. In order to change it you must own it. Personal growth comes from the day-to-day process of making choices—positive and negative. Stop blaming others, and begin to own your thoughts and choices.

✔ **Stop trying to be perfect!**

Is perfection a reality? Do you know anyone who is perfect?

Accept yourself. This includes your talents, strengths, flaws, and imperfections. Embrace yourself for who you are and who you want to become. Appreciate all aspects of yourself, be true to yourself, and stop blaming yourself for past mistakes. Stop trying to be perfect, and don't pretend to be someone or something that you're not.

✔ Stop letting others control you!

Do you allow others to control your inner GPS?

Take control of your life and destination by moving into the driver's seat. Give up on relationships—personal or professional—that encourage you to be someone or something that you're not. When other people tell you that *you can't do this or that because it is too difficult or impossible,* stop listening! Learn to listen to your inner voice and to trust in your instincts. Take control of your inner GPS, and stop letting others control you.

✔ Stop the negative self-talk!

What messages are you sending to yourself? Are your thoughts and feelings positive or negative?

You are what you think, and all actions begin as a thought. Stop sending negative messages to yourself about yourself. Begin to focus on the positives about yourself, your abilities, and your life. If you want to live a happy, healthy, successful life, think happy, healthy, successful thoughts. Begin each day with thoughts that promote confidence, security, and stability, and stop the negative self-talk. One way to help is to wear a rubber band on your wrist. Every time you catch yourself thinking negative thoughts about yourself, snap the band! Ouch! That sting will remind you not do it again!

✔ Stop feeling entitled!

Do you think that the world owes you?

No, the world does not owe you anything! A sense of entitlement promotes feelings of unhappiness, low motivation, and disrespect. Hard work is a strong predictor of happiness. Learn to work and to enjoy it. Stop feeling entitled and begin to recognize that the real solution to a successful life comes from hard work and gratitude.

Stop the stream of negative thoughts and alter your mindset. Shift your perspective with prompts that promote healthy thoughts. Distance yourself from black-and-white thinking, and don't get embedded in negative emotions. Focus on the positive aspects of your life and current situations. Control what you can, and let go of what you can't change.

> *No pessimist ever discovered the secrets of the stars, or sailed to an uncharted land, or opened a new heaven to the human spirit.*
>
> *—Helen Keller*

Avoid Distractions

Distractions are a part of daily life, and technology is often the driving force behind many distractions. Research tells us that 85 percent of Americans feel uncomfortable with technology, and employees are interrupted at least three hours a day by technology devices and tools. Is the buzzing of your cell phone and beep of each new text message or email distracting you?

Here are a few ideas to help you minimize the disruptions in your life:

Attention is limited. Attempting to accomplish two or more tasks at once causes you to divide your attention. We have a limited capacity for processing information. It is impossible to attend to, remember, or respond to everything we encounter. This limited capacity plays a vital role with attention, and we allocate our attention to the tasks we are focused on. Focus on less, and tune your attention to the important, appropriate task. Turn off your cell phone during meetings, check your messages a few times a day, and return emails in the morning, not throughout the day. This will help you eliminate distractions, concentrate, and successfully accomplish tasks at home and in the work environment.

Multitasking is a myth. Effective multitasking is a myth and so is the idea that we can concentrate on several things at one time. Research shows that you may be an excellent multi-tasker for a certain set of tasks, but that does not mean you can successfully multi-task at everything with ease. It is important to know your limits and recognize the mind's limited capacity for attention and focus. You will feel frustrated, and your performance will deteriorate when you attempt to focus on many tasks at one time.

Identify high-peak performance time. Identify time in your day when you are at your optimum. This is the time you feel most awake, energetic and focused. Identify this time slot as your peak performance time, and reserve it for the high priority, time-consuming, complex tasks.

Don't leave the worst for last. Too often we place the enjoyable, innovative tasks at the top of our list and leave the tedious, less motivating tasks for the bottom of the list. This is not an effective strategy. Do the tedious, mundane tasks early in the day, and get them out of the way. It is difficult to address these tasks at the end of the day when your energy and focus are at a low point.

Memory paralysis. We have a lot to attend to and remember in a given day and it is impossible to remember everything. We cannot process or remember all sources of information, so it is important to jot down relevant information. Two lists that are helpful and drive success are—an **"action" list** and an **"idea" list.**

- ✔ A daily action list will be highly effective when all tasks are itemized by importance and priority. Recognize that a list of many items is not realistic or attainable.

- ✔ An idea list is used to jot down productive, creative or insightful thoughts that may be useful down the road. It is much easier to retrieve important information and insights from an idea list and not rely on memory alone.

Each day we have moments when we're distracted and lack motivation. Minimize daily disruptions in your life by attending to the important tasks during your peak performance time. Focus and engage during meetings and conversations by turning down the volume on your cell phone. Set aside time in your day to return text messages and emails. Learn to effectively manage your time, and don't allow technology to trap you and minimize your productivity.

Close the Door on Failure

Some days are difficult, and others are not. Too often we focus on the difficult days, allowing the positive days in life to be overlooked and easily forgotten. Close the door on setbacks and failure by focusing on seven key points that will inspire optimism and success.

Focus on the lesson. Frustrating, difficult situations are a part of our personal and professional lives. At first setbacks appear to be failures that create feelings of discouragement—but even setbacks have a silver lining if we take the time to identify them. Each day, life offers us opportunities to learn and grow. It is critical to look for the lesson in each experience and learn from it. Appreciate and embrace opportunities for growth. The process of learning helps us to be adaptable and more resilient—two qualities necessary for success.

Play it safe. Often life is about taking risks and requires you to step outside of your comfort zone. On the other hand, playing it safe can also be valuable advice. Prior to taking risks, play it safe by ensuring that your action plan is attainable. Explore all your options, do your homework, recognize your strengths, and understand your limitations. Forward progression requires risk, but playing it safe is also wise advice.

Choose to control. Life's challenges can promote feelings of despair. When you feel overwhelmed, it is tempting to give up and let someone else take charge of your life. This is the easy way out and is a temporary fix to your problems. Allowing others to "drive" your life leaves you feeling hopeless and out of control. When you turn over control to others, you give up on yourself and your personal goals. Determine the direction in your life by identifying what's important to you. Drive these goals by setting personal boundaries and being focused. Choose to control your life and drive success on your terms.

Don't give up. Some days it seems easier to throw in the towel and give up on life. Resentment, criticism, and pessimism promote feelings of negativity and prevent optimism, hope, and happiness.

Let go of resentment—forgive yourself and others. Leave hostility behind you and move forward freeing yourself from bitterness.

Criticism promotes negative feelings and actions. Judging yourself and others is a waste of your time and energy. Focus on the positive attributes in yourself and others, and feel free from excuses and failures.

Avoid pessimism by looking on the bright side of life. Stop dreaming about your goals and take action. Focus on giving yourself credit instead of discrediting your talents and abilities. Give yourself a second chance when setbacks occur. Embrace opportunities with optimism—not pessimism.

Happiness and success are found not only in positivity but in reality. Life is not going to be a hundred percent blissful all of the time, and life without some struggle is not reality. Life can be compared to a roller coaster ride, with ups and downs, bends, and twists. The joy of the ride comes from the twists and turns, the ups and downs. Enduring and enjoying the ride is what opens the door to success and closes the door on failure.

Success Comes in All Sizes

Success is the progressive realization of a worthwhile goal. It is important to recognize that success comes in all sizes. Success to one may be measured by money and to another it is measured through contributions of time and service. Success varies from one person to the next based on individual perspectives, values, and motives.

Too often we see success as the end result, the finale. Success is also the steps leading up to the finale. It is participating in and running the race—not just crossing the finish line.

Six steps to achieving success personally and professionally:

- ✔ **Hard work.** You choose success. Hard work makes success a reality. Believe in your vision, stay focused, and work at succeeding.

  "One can never consent to creep when one has the impulse to soar."—Helen Keller

- ✔ **Take action.** Nothing gets accomplished by standing still. Forward progression relies on action steps.

  "Action is the foundational key to all success."—Pablo Picasso

- ✔ **Have passion and be persistent.** Choose what you love and love what you choose. Be persistent when faced with challenges and discouragement. Combine passion with persistence, and success will follow. Most important, love what you do.

  "Don't aim for success if you want it; just do what you love and believe in, and it will come naturally."—David Frost

- ✔ **Listen and observe.** Learn from others. Be a good listener, and be willing to take advice from those who have insights and wisdom that you don't have.

"Always bear in mind that your own resolution to succeed is more important than any other."—Abraham Lincoln

✔ **Learn from failure.** View failure as an opportunity to learn—not as an excuse to quit.

"Failure is a success if we learn from it."—Malcolm Forbes

✔ **Criticism can motivate.** Avoid looking at criticism as defeat or reason to doubt yourself. Allow criticism to be a motivator.

"A successful man is one who can lay a firm foundation with the bricks others throw at him."—David Brinkley

"Success comes in CANs—not CAN'Ts." Great insights shared by my mom. I got tired of hearing it as a teenager and would roll my eyes each time she expressed these words of wisdom. Now as an adult, I appreciate her advice. It's the truth!

Planted to Bloom

In the spring, I enjoy planting seeds in my garden. I carefully place each seed deep into the rich, brown soil with the expectation that it will bloom. Seeds are planted to bloom. People can also bloom in a metaphorical sense.

The definition of bloom is *to grow or flourish*. Personal *growth* requires hard work and is a life-long process. To *flourish* is to thrive, a sense of accomplishment resulting from hard work and discipline.

Many people view happiness and success as having it all, everything that life offers. The world's evolving concept of "he or she who has the most wins" does not bring true happiness. It's not wealth, beauty or superior intelligence that brings happiness. True happiness is achieved through hard work, involvement in a loving relationship, and a sense of belonging.

"Blooming" begins by knowing yourself, who you are and what you want out of life. Knowing who you are is important but knowing where you are headed in life is essential.

- ✔ **Create your identity.** Choose to be strong mentally and physically. Exercise and eat a healthy diet. Build your confidence by recognizing your worth, learning to handle rejection, and exercising self-discipline.

- ✔ **Dare to dream big.** What seems impossible is often possible. Believe in yourself and your abilities. Focus on your strengths, and choose positive thoughts.

- ✔ **Step out of your comfort zone.** Forward progression requires movement. You must be willing to change, transition, and take action. Persevere, and take the time to recognize all your successes—even the small ones.

- ✔ **Accept praise.** Too often an initial response to a sincere compliment might be to deflect the praise. David Dunning, PhD, professor of psychology at Cornell University claims that people are more likely to remember betrayals than positive interactions. Individuals underestimate other's sincerity and generosity. Allow praise to boost your self-esteem by embracing compliments and viewing them as sincere and generous.

- ✔ **Move forward with confidence.** You choose your self-concept, the mental picture of yourself. See yourself as confident, competent, and capable.

To flourish is to grow well, to thrive, and prosper. Flourishing is the end result; it's to achieve success. The process of achievement requires clarity, focus, effort, and persistence. Seeds are planted to bloom, to flourish, and so are you!

*When I look into the future,
it is so bright it burns my eyes.
—Oprah Winfrey*

You are your own best RESOURCE.

Realize your potential

Endure challenges and change

Success comes in CANs not CAN'Ts

Optimism impacts reality

Unlimited is your potential

Rely on your instincts

Clarify your goals

Esteem from within

Empowerment Logic for Children and Teens

Parents need to fill a child's bucket of self-esteem so high that the rest of the world can't poke enough holes to drain it dry.

—Alvin Price

PUZZLE PIECES IN THIS SECTION:

Be a Champion!

Build self-esteem in children and teens

Self-esteem is your opinion of yourself. It begins with your self-concept or mental picture. There is a lot of truth in the phrase, *we are what we think*. Therefore, high self-esteem is a good opinion of one's self resulting from positive thoughts. Low self-esteem is a poor opinion of one's self resulting from negative thoughts. It all begins with how you see yourself and whether you like what you see.

Self-esteem is critical for attaining success. It is the cornerstone of positive choices, a healthy attitude towards life, and the reaching of one's potential. Patterns of self-esteem begin early in life as a child tries to master new skills—crawling, standing, sitting, and walking. Children, who are happy with their achievements, are applauded for their successes, feel loved, and experience healthy self-esteem.

Help foster healthy self-esteem in children and teens by following these steps:

✔ **Teach by example.** Be positive about your own abilities and successes. Avoid being harsh and critical about your personal limitations and failures.

✔ **Watch your words.** Take time to praise kids for their accomplishments. Focus on the effort and not the outcome. When it is necessary to correct behavior, be honest, direct, and consistent. Avoid the use of demeaning and condescending words. Use the "5-to-1" ratio. Share five positive comments for every one negative.

✔ **Give hugs and compliments.** Share your feelings of praise and love with children and teens. Never skimp on compliments. Be realistic and truthful; kids can sense if you're not being sincere.

✔ **Help kids be rational.** Children and teens can be their own worst critics and view themselves in an irrational way.

Help them to be honest and accurate while evaluating their strengths and weaknesses. Teach them skills to manage or change their vulnerabilities while showing gratitude for their strengths and talents.

✔ **Keep communication open.** Allow youth to express their feelings and opinions without sharing your critical feedback. Respect their opinion, be a good listener, and encourage opportunities for them to self-advocate.

Promote a healthy self-image and build confidence in children and teens by creating a safe environment, involving them in activities that promote cooperation rather than competition, and sharing empowering messages.

> *I always surprise myself on my ability to turn a phrase. Words are, in my not so humble opinion, the most inexhaustible source of magic; capable of both inflicting injury and remedying it.*
> —Albus Dumbledore, Harry Potter

Power Words

Is your child struggling with self-esteem?

Teach children to feel empowered and confident by helping them recognize that they have control over their self-concept. A self-concept is a collection of beliefs about one's behavior and unique qualities. In other words, your self-concept is your own mental picture of yourself. It is a collection of self-perceptions.

The verbal and non-verbal messages your children believes about themselves, affect their self-concept. Teach children to avoid these three words: **"I will try."** "I will try" gives them permission to fail or to avoid commitment. Teach them to feel confident and capable by using three power words: **"I will do."** Self-esteem will increase when your child's mental picture is healthy and positive. Take the time to EMPOWER your son or daughter!

The Techno-Mania Craze

Tweens and teens have embraced and absorbed our ever-changing world of technology. Blogging, texting, tweeting, and Facebook are all a part of the social network boom. It is critical that youth learn to control technology and not allow it to control them.

Technology can create stress for teens and their families. Techno-stress is your reaction to technology and how it is changing one's life. Technostress affects teens and their relationships. Many families get into their techno-cocoons with one family member texting, the other playing a video game and yet another watching a high-definition television set. The result of this scenario is a lack of communication among family members.

Five ideas to help teens control technology:

✔ **Teach teens to exercise self-discipline.**

Set specific FAMILY rules and boundaries in regard to technology and on-line use. Be clear about the expectations and consequences. Teach teens self-discipline through personal example. If the family rule is no cell phones while driving, don't let your teen catch you sneaking a look at your phone while driving.

✔ **Teach teens that an imbalanced life is the result of making poor choices.**

Empower teens by teaching them to own their choices and the consequences of each choice.

✔ **Teach teens to plan ahead and avoid procrastination.**

Allow teens to make important decisions regarding their own schedules and to learn from the consequences of effective and ineffective time management.

✔ **Teach teens to minimize distractions in their world.**

Teens will be empowered when they learn to control their use of technology.

✔ **Encourage teens to have face-to-face relationships.**

Self-belief and confidence will increase as teens improve their communication and social skills.

The bottom line is parents cannot be with their teens 24/7. It is important to teach them that balancing their lifestyle and managing social media is a personal CHOICE! Teach teens to take control of technological tools rather than being controlled by them. Set rules that will limit the use of technological tools. Begin by setting aside at least fifteen minutes each day for family time. Limit the use of cell phones at the dinner table, and encourage face-to-face communication and interaction. Help teens decrease technostress in their lives by exercising control when it comes to the use of technology.

Is Bullying REAL?

What is bullying?

Bullying is a form of aggressive behavior. It is acting in ways that demean, scare, threaten, or harm another person. Bullying can happen anywhere and to anyone.

Bullying is a serious problem in our society. Kids who are bullied tend to feel helpless, angry, anxious, and even depressed and suicidal.

Boys and girls both bully. Girls generally bully in emotional ways by gossiping and through exclusion. Boys use emotional and physical means to bully by name calling, taunting, shoving and pushing others. Cyber-bullying is also used by both boys and girls. Cyber-bullying is using high-tech devices, such as texting and Facebook, to spread rumors or send hurtful messages and pictures.

Who is the bully?

Children and teens who bully are often looking for ways to feel and act powerful. They are often impulsive and may bully because they have been bullied by others, perhaps even at home. Bullies are often physically strong and do not have regard for others feelings. Kids who bully are more likely to drop out of school, use drugs and alcohol and break the law. Children who bully need professional counseling.

How can bullying be stopped?

Children often feel scared and angry when they are bullied, which often allows the bullying to continue. Help children stop bullying by following these four steps:

- ✔ Teach kids to speak up. Using assertive, not aggressive, communication is the key. Assertiveness is the ability to speak honestly and directly without being angry or anxious.

  Examples of assertive communication are: "Leave me alone." "Do not push me."

- ✔ Walk away from the bully. Do not run. Running can escalate the situation and turn into a chase.

- ✔ Tell an adult.

- ✔ Encourage children and teens to help other kids from being bullied. Teach them not to turn away from those being bullied, or to participate as a spectator. Kids need to take action. Omission is not the solution.

Resource: www.bullybeware.com

Bullying is REAL

77% of students are bullied mentally, verbally and/or physically.

What's the risk of being bullied at school?

- ✔ Bullying begins in elementary school, peaks in middle school, and falls off in high school. It does not, however, disappear altogether. (*The Facts About Bullying*, 1997)

- ✔ 61.6% of students who are bullied are picked on because of their looks or speech. (*U.S. News & World Report*, May 7, 2001)

- ✔ Of the students who are bullied, 55.6% report being hit, slapped or pushed. (*U.S. News & World Report*, May 7, 2001)

How do students react to bullying?

- ✔ Up to 7% of eighth grade students stay home at least once a month because of bullies.

- ✔ In a 1993 survey of students, 6-12 grades, 50% knew someone that changed schools to feel safer. (National School Safety Center)

- ✔ More than 42% of middle and high school students avoid using school bathrooms for fear of being harassed or assaulted. (*Mothering*, May/June 2001)

- ✔ One in fifteen students said they avoided certain places at school because they feared being attacked. (Harvard School of Public Health)

- ✔ By age 24, 60% of identified bullies have a criminal conviction.

Cyber Bullying Statistics

- • 42% of kids have been bullied online.

- • 35% of kids have been threatened online.

- • 21% of kids have received mean or threatening emails or other messages.

- 58% of kids admit someone has said mean or hurtful things to them online.

- 53% of kids have not told their parents or an adult about something mean or hurtful that happened to them online.

(Based on 2004 I-Safe survey of 1,500 students grades 4-8)

Take action!

Watch for signs of abuse, problems in school, troubles with peers, and other factors that affect children and teen's self-esteem and confidence. Deal with these issues in a sensitive, private, and honest manner. Respect kid's opinions, concerns, and fears. Do not downplay the situation or view it as unimportant. Help kids feel good about themselves while dealing with conflict and resisting negative peer pressure. Seek professional counseling if necessary.

The Perfect Combination: Children and Advocacy

When children are young, we, their parents, are their greatest advocates. Our kids will grow up and, at some point, need to advocate for themselves. They will not automatically have self-advocacy skills when they turn eighteen and leave for college or begin a new job.

It is important that children learn to advocate for themselves about themselves. The following steps will help teach children to advocate.

1. Allow children to have a voice. Do not speak for them.

2. Value children's opinion and encourage it to be heard.

3. Help children to recognize their strengths.

4. Teach children to set personal boundaries with themselves and others.

5. Teach children to problem-solve and think for themselves.

Teaching children to have a voice and to speak up about their needs and wants will increase their confidence. Effective advocacy skills will help children to feel capable and empowered.

CONNECT with your Daughter

The mother-daughter bond sets the stage for both physical and emotional well-being. We not only inherit our mothers' DNA, but a child's core beliefs about life, health, and what's possible are in place by age ten.
—Dr. Christiane Northrup, MD

Girls who feel competent can cope with life's challenges better than those who think they are inept. Self-assurance also allows girls to take the risks necessary to learn and grow. For your daughter to become strong, feel good about who she is, and draw upon her inner resources, she must get to know herself, think of herself as capable, and believe she can measure up to others' expectations. Mothers play an important role in this process.
—Dr. Roni Cohen-Sandler, PhD

Why Connect?

According to the latest research, the mother-daughter connection…

- ✔ is vital to a girl's physical and emotional health;
- ✔ influences thriving conditions for girls: confidence, competence, connection, caring, and contribution;
- ✔ prevents alcohol, tobacco, and drug use and risky sexual behavior;
- ✔ clears up confusing messages about girls' bodies and their abilities.

Six social trends affecting the connection between mother and daughter:

- ✔ the economy—the more hours at work, the less time with the children;

✔ increased stress—worries over money and work causing trickle down anxiety and withdrawal in children;

✔ over-scheduling—parents and children overly involved in a variety of activities with little or no time left over for one-on-one connection;

✔ technology—cell phones and social media have taken the place of real face time;

✔ parents afraid to be parents—the "forever young" script for parents today has left kids without boundaries and connections;

✔ emotionally detached children—due to the lack of time spent with a trusted caregiver children have downsized their emotional expectations, resulting in detachment.

Six Ways to Connect

Make the choice to:

✔ Invest time—commit to ten minutes of uninterrupted time a day to spend with your daughter.

✔ Appreciate her gifts—step back by assessing your own emotional needs so that your daughter can step up and realize her unique talents and abilities.

✔ Emphasize her strengths—catch your daughter being good.

✔ Nurture her passions—help her set realistic goals.

✔ Evaluate her stress—ask your daughter directly how she feels and what she needs from you.

✔ Start a mother-daughter connection tradition—choose an activity you both enjoy and do it together regularly.

Make the time to CONNECT with your daughter!

I cannot forget my mother. She is my BRIDGE.
When I needed to get across, she steadied herself
long enough for me to run across safely.
-Renita Weems

Help Your Daughter THRIVE

Mothers play a key role in developing a successful connection with their daughters.

The most important thing a mother can do to teach her daughter how to "make sense out of the world" is to spend time bonding with her daughter, especially at an early age.

Mothers are ROLE models for their daughters.

A mother's beliefs and behaviors influence her daughter's thoughts and actions. This has more power and influence than any other factor in her life.

Three important things a mother can do for her daughter are:
 ✔ connect with her;
 ✔ empower her with confidence and self-belief;
 ✔ believe in the relationship she and her daughter share.

CONNECTING
♥ **Life is so busy. I have trouble finding time to connect with my daughter.**

Regardless of your daughter's age, finding time to connect with her can be a challenge. Invest time by committing at least ten minutes of uninterrupted time a day to spend with your daughter. If you have other children or even other daughters, do not include them in your "special time." Treat each child as an individual. Start a mother-daughter connection tradition. Set the time, write it on the family calendar and keep the appointment. Choose an activity you both enjoy and do it regularly. Make connecting with your daughter a *priority*.

HEALTH
♥ **My daughter seems to struggle with life's stresses. How can I help her manage stress?**

✔ Be a positive role model by managing stress in your own life.

✔ Help her feel competent and confident. Girls who feel competent and confident can cope with life's stresses better than those who do not.

✔ Address her stress. Don't be afraid to ask her directly how she feels or what she needs from you.

✔ Teach her to self-advocate by recognizing her feelings and expressing them.

THRIVE
♥ **My daughter seems to have little belief in herself. How can I help her to feel more confident?**

✔ Teach her to empower herself from within by focusing on inner qualities, not external sources.

✔ Encourage her to recognize and appreciate her gifts and talents.

✔ Help her to become strong, feel good about who she is and draw upon her inner sources by…
  1. getting to know herself;
  2. thinking of herself as capable;
  3. believing that she is able to measure up to other's expectations.

PREVENT

♥ **When I try to talk with my daughter about drugs and alcohol, she seems uninterested and tunes me out. How can I communicate effectively with her?**

When it comes to dangerous substances, don't assume your daughter knows where you stand. She may act bored or like she isn't listening, but she is hearing you, so keep talking. Your opinions about drugs, alcohol, and risky sexual behavior matter significantly when it comes to the choices your daughter will make.

- ✔ Make time to talk in a distraction-free environment.

- ✔ Set clear rules and include the consequences if rules are not followed.

- ✔ Stay involved in her life, tell her how you will be doing this, and *know her friends.*

- ✔ Allow her time to voice her opinion and share her feelings.

- ✔ Do not preach. Be positive but firm.

CONFUSING MESSAGES

♥ **There are many mixed messages out there. How can I help my daughter feel good about her body and abilities?**

- ✔ Feel positive about <u>your</u> body. Your daughter looks to you for advice and sees you as an example on healthy living. My friend shared with me that she overheard her nine year-old daughter complaining about her body and weight. She realized that her daughter was mimicking her and was developing a poor body image at a very young age.

- ✔ Promote a healthy body image by teaching your daughter to appreciate her body for what it does and not how it looks.

- ✔ Teach your daughter to focus on inner qualities, and not outward appearance.

✔ Help your daughter understand that happiness is cultivated by accepting herself, appreciating her abilities, and discovering her inner strengths.

Building a strong mother-daughter relationship will help your daughter develop a positive, optimistic attitude towards herself, her abilities, and her outlook on life. A healthy self-esteem and lifestyle are a great combination that leads to successful living.

RECYCLE "Common Sense" Messages

Recycling is processing used materials into new products to prevent waste of potentially useful materials. Take time to recycle these six common sense messages and empower your children to feel capable and competent… You may learn from these messages and feel empowered, too!

1. **Message: You are what you think.**

Thoughts are POWERFUL.

It is not possible to have negative and positive thoughts simultaneously. OPTIMISM is to expect good outcomes. Optimism lessens the impact of stress and creates feelings of hope and belief. Optimists are more likely to engage in action-oriented, problem-solving behavior.

> **Example:** Prior to the tryout for the school basketball team, encourage your children to focus on their strengths, not their weaknesses, and to visualize a positive outcome—not a negative one.

> "When you tryout today for the basketball team, focus on your amazing ability to dribble the ball with both hands. See yourself shooting a three point basket. You will be awesome!"

2.   **Message: Choose the RIGHT choice not the good choice.**

Good choices vs. RIGHT choices

The RIGHT choice is not always the fun choice, but it is always the BEST choice.

Correct choices build self-esteem and increase confidence.

> **Example:** Help your child recognize which choice is the right choice as opposed to the good choice by asking them to evaluate the options.
>
> "Which choice is the right choice: going to the school basketball game with friends or staying at home to study for your algebra test?"

3.   **Message: When the going gets tough, it may be best to laugh about it.**

Humor is a STRESS Reliever.

Research shows that humor lessens the impact of stress. Humor can help people bounce back from defeats, disappointments, and embarrassment. Humor increases positive emotions. Parents are role models for their children when it comes to coping with stress.

> **Example:** Your daughter comes home from school and expresses her frustration from striking out while playing baseball during recess. Put a less threatening spin on the situation with humor.
>
> "Let's look at the bright side. As a ballerina, you don't need to be great at swinging a bat—you can balance on your toes!"

4.   **Message: You are capable!**

Promote feelings of competence.

For children to become strong, feel good about who they are, and draw upon their inner resources, they must do the following:

✔ know themselves;

✔ see themselves as capable;

✔ believe they can meet other's expectations.

> **Example:** Take time to point out positive behavior, helping children to see they can meet others' expectations. Your son expresses doubts about his ability to play a solo on his clarinet for the school play. He recognizes that his teacher is counting on him to do a good job.

> "You are prepared, and you have practiced hard. You will do a great job. I know Mr. Smith will be pleased with your performance."

5.   **Message: You CONTROL yourself—not others.**

ADVOCACY skills help children set personal boundaries.

Self-advocacy is to understand your strengths and needs and to effectively communicate them to others.

Benefits of Self Advocacy:

✔ avoid and solve problems with family, friends;

✔ make informed decisions concerning personal choices;

✔ gain essential tools for defining and resolving problems;

✔ set boundaries with peers.

> **Example:** Teach children to speak up for themselves by not speaking for them. During a visit to the doctor encourage your child to speak to the doctor about their health.

> "You are not feeling well? Explain to the doctor how you are feeling."

6.   **Message: The key to happiness is hard work.**

A strong predictor of happiness is working hard.

Teach children to work hard and to do a good job for themselves and others. This will promote happiness.

Example: Use positive language with yourself and your children about hard work, and participate in service projects as a family. Make service fun!

"On Saturday we will be helping with the community clean-up project. This will be a great opportunity for our family. After the clean-up we will get pizza."

Reinforce these common sense messages and help youth feel confident, competent, and capable.

Personal Best

Boost your daughter's confidence

How does your daughter see herself? What does her mental picture of herself look like?

To boost your daughter's confidence it is important to take a close look at her self-esteem.

Self-esteem is how she feels about herself. It's a self-evaluation. Her self-esteem influences all aspects of her life. Teens with high self-esteem know themselves well, feel in control of their lives, find friends easily, and appreciate who they are. For teens with low self-esteem, just the opposite is true. They don't recognize their own strengths or feel positive about their abilities. They struggle to find friends and are unrealistic about their lives and future.

In Western cultures, girls' self-esteem declines significantly during adolescence. As their bodies begin to change, their self-esteem begins to decrease. Sociocultural factors, such as unrealistic pictures of ultra-thin magazine models and other media images account for this distortion and decline in esteem. The world glorifies the "perfect body." It is difficult for your daughter to see the positives about her own body when the world is telling her that perfection is the goal.

Body image is how your daughter views her physical appearance.

Does your daughter see herself as too tall, too short, too thin, or too heavy? Is she putting herself down for how she looks? If you answered yes to any of these questions, you are not alone. Most teens fall into this trap of negatives. In order to change negative thoughts into positive ones, help your daughter focus on the good points about her appearance.

Teach her to look at her body as healthy, appreciating how it functions—not how it looks. Tell her that her body is unique, and encourage her to appreciate it. A poor opinion of her body will lower her self-esteem, and she will feel less capable of achieving her personal goals.

Self-esteem and body image are important because they influence how your daughter feels about herself. They can affect her mental health and behavior.

Here are ten tips to help raise self-esteem and improve body image:

- ✔ Focus on the positives about your body and recognize the features that you like.

- ✔ Accept yourself for who you are and not the way you look.

- ✔ Compliment yourself on something other than your appearance.

- ✔ View your body as healthy, and stop apologizing for how you look.

- ✔ Wear clothes that make you feel good about yourself.

- ✔ Exercise, and stop looking at foods as good or bad. Think of food as healthy or unhealthy.

- ✔ Set realistic goals, and reward yourself for your successes.

- ✔ Listen to your body, and respond to its needs.

✔ Avoid reading/watching/listening to media sources that make you feel badly about yourself.

✔ Do not allow others to dictate what body type is acceptable for you.

Encourage your daughter to choose to have a positive body image. This will help to increase her self-esteem. Teach her to like and accept herself for who she is and to recognize her worth. It is important that she does not try to fit the media "ideal". It is best to focus on having a healthy attitude about her body and how it functions. Encourage her to avoid friends who decrease her self-worth by putting her down or asking her to be someone she's not. Remind your daughter that, true friends will love and accept her for who she is, not for who they want her to be.

Knowing herself, recognizing what makes her happy and how to achieve her goals will help your daughter feel esteemed, capable, strong and in control of her life. Teach her to focus on her personal best and to invite happiness into her life.

Male Call

Boost confidence in boys

Girls and their body image are a major focus in today's society but guess what? When it comes to body image, boys care too! The focus on a perfect body is no longer just a "girl" thing. All adolescents worry about how they look, appear to their friends, and compare to others. Boys and girls want to look like models, superstars, and TV pop idols.

Boys pay close attention to professional athletes and their physically fit bodies. Unlike girls, however, most boys aren't out to get skinny. They want to bulk up and some are going to extreme efforts to get muscular physiques. Unfortunately, most teens believe that they are not attractive if they don't look like models, athletes, and celebrities.

I have watched my own two sons worry about how big and strong they are. They believe in the stereotype of being tall, strong, and handsome. Over the past thirty years, the ideal male physique has become more muscular. Boys are often influenced negatively by messages from the media about looking and feeling powerful.

Boys who have a poor self-image also suffer from low self-esteem, and fall short of their potential. We can help boys recognize that fitting within the boundaries of the media "ideal" is not the goal. Liking and accepting themselves will help them to feel empowered.

Here are a few tips to help boys develop a healthy body image:

- ✔ **Emphasize the importance of health**. Begin at an early age to teach boys about eating healthily and getting lots of exercise. Help boys resist "fads" and extreme dieting messages by fostering a healthy lifestyle for all those in your household.

- ✔ **Focus on health over looks**. Maintain ongoing encouragement with the boys in your care about what their bodies do rather than the way they look. And don't forget to set a great example yourself.

- ✔ **Encourage honest dialogue**. Be open with your son about your personal feelings and experience concerning body image. Let your son know that you understand and that he is welcome to talk to you about it anytime. This can be the beginning of a life-long dialogue.

- ✔ **Develop an active family lifestyle**. Spend time together in activities that promote fitness and good health. Begin by turning off the TV, and encourage boys to manage their screen time.

- ✔ **Keep an eye on your boys' online activity.** Social networks and texts carry some risks because boys can fuel their obsession in isolation. Risky bodybuilding training, and unattainable body ideals can be found and pursued without adult approval.

- ✔ **Do a reality check about sports teams.** If your son participates in sports, find out what kind of messages are being shared by coaches, training staff, and other team members. Make sure the program is designed to promote the larger goal of being healthy and is not just about winning.

- ✔ **Check your own behavior and messages.** What messages are you sending to your son about body image? Are you overly critical of your own body? Do you eat well and exercise? Teach by example, and engage in a healthy lifestyle for yourself.

Encourage young men to focus on the health of their bodies rather than their physical attributes. Teach them to eat healthy foods, to exercise, and to maintain their personal hygiene, and cleanliness. Involvement in sports like soccer, baseball or basketball, will also help them to feel stronger, and physically fit. Being a part of teams, and clubs will give them a sense of belonging, and increase their confidence.

Navigating through adolescence is a challenge for all teens. Help young men to accept themselves, focus on their strengths, take control of their thoughts and actions, and value themselves. Boys are affected by the media's standard of perfection. Encourage them to attain their own ideal, to feel esteemed and capable of reaching their potential.

The CHALLENGES?

I have always grown from my problems and challenges—from things that don't work out— that's when I've really learned.
—Carol Burnett

Challenges make you discover things about yourself that you really never knew. They're what make the instrument stretch—what make you go beyond the norm.
—Cicely Tyson

The ANSWERS.

Arrange whatever pieces come your way.
—Virginia Woolf

I think the one lesson I have learned is that there is no substitute for paying attention.
—Diane Sawyer

The way I see it, if you want the rainbow, you gotta put up with the rain.
—Dolly Parton

...As long as one keeps searching, the answers come.
—Joan Baez

I am not afraid of storms for I am learning how to sail my own ship.
—Louisa May Alcott

The REWARDS!

Reach high, for stars lie hidden in your soul.
Dream deep, for every dream proceeds the goal.
—Pamela Vaull Starr

The mere sense of living is joy enough.
—Emily Dickinson

Life isn't about waiting for the storm to pass...It's
about learning to dance in the rain.
—Vivian Greene

Conclusion

Opportunities to build your "personal puzzle" happen each day. Life experiences create the momentum of building. You have the choice to participate in positive building or negative building. Positive building creates feelings of confidence and happiness. Negative building results in low self-esteem and unhappiness.

The challenge of the building process is to embrace opportunities to make change in your life. Change is difficult; it forces you out of your "comfort zone." The decision to make change is met with resistance, but is necessary for personal growth.

Missing and misplaced pieces in your "personal puzzle" will cause imbalances preventing you from reaching your potential personally and professionally. Take the time to identify the missing pieces. The strategies and insights from this book will assist you in the life-long process of puzzle building.

We **all** have missing puzzle pieces. It's what we choose to do about it that allows us to grow. Increased confidence, clarity, and success will be attained as you choose to identify and place the missing pieces in your "personal puzzle."

Suggested Reading List

This list contains books that will uplift and inspire you to feel confident, capable, and motivated to live a successful life.

A Million Miles in a Thousand Years: How I Learned To Live a Better Story by Donald Miller

All I Really Needed to Know I Learned in Kindergarten by Robert Fulghum

Aspire: Discovering Your Purpose Through the Power of Words by Kevin Hall and Stephen R. Covey

First Things First by Stephen Covey

How We Decide by Jonah Lehrer

Lincoln on Leadership by Donald T. Phillips

Outliers: The Story of Success by Malcolm Gladwell

Team of Rivals: The Political Genius of Abraham Lincoln by Doris Kearns Goodwin

Rent Collector by Cameron Wright

The Boys in the Boat: Nine Americans & Their Epic Quest for Gold and the 1936 Berlin Olympics by Daniel James Brown

The Book Thief by Markus Zusak

The Heart of a Leader by Ken Blanchard

Unbroken: A World War II Story of Survival by Laura Hillenbrand

Wild: From Lost to Found on the Crest Trail by Cheryl Strayed

Your Thoughts, Change Your Life by Dr. Wayne Dyer

About the Author

Vikki is a highly sought after author and national speaker. She is a master at motivating and empowering diverse audiences. Vikki's innovative approach is strategy-driven and based on the latest professional development trends. She is highly effective at helping individuals identify their resistance level to change, overcome roadblocks to their success, decrease stress and increase personal and professional productivity.

Vikki is the president of Vikki Carrel and Company, the creator of The Empowerment Project, author of *Switching Lanes*, and co-author of *Chloe's Closet*. While living back East, she co-founded Two Balance, Inc. and Mother Daughter America—a national movement to re-connect mothers and daughters.

Vikki has conducted seminars across the United States in both the private and public sectors for well-known companies and organizations like Verizon, Capital Health System, and Temple University, and she is a frequent contributor on regional and national television.

Prior to the development of Two Balance, Inc. Vikki was the co-owner of a Texas-based fashion production company. She worked in the fashion industry for fifteen years producing events for the likes of Olivia Newton John, *GQ Magazine*, and designers Steve Fabrikant and Ralph Lauren.

Vikki holds a degree in business administration/marketing. She and her husband have two grown sons, and they live in the heart of the Utah Rocky Mountains.

Join the conversation and learn more at vikkicarrel.com.

www.ingramcontent.com/pod-product-compliance
Lightning Source LLC
LaVergne TN
LVHW021453080426
835509LV00018B/2272